THE MESSENGER OF ALLAH
A BIOGRAPHY OF MUHAMMAD RASULULLAH
(Salla Allahu Alaihi Wa Sallam)

SENIOR LEVEL — PART II
Textbook

IQRA' PROGRAM OF SÎRAH

Part of

*A Comprehensive and Systematic Program of
Islamic Studies*

Abidullah al-Ansari Ghazi
Ph.D. Harvard
Tasneema Khatoon Ghazi
Ph.D. Minnesota

IQRA' INTERNATIONAL EDUCATIONAL FOUNDATION
Chicago

Part of a Comprehensive and Systematic Program of Islamic Studies

A Textbook for
the Program of Sirah
Senior Level

The Messenger of Allah Textbook: Part Two

Chief Program Editors
Dr. Abidullah al-Ansari Ghazi
Ph.D., Harvard University

Tasneema Khatoon Ghazi
Ph.D., University of Minnesota

Religious Review
Rabita al-Alam al-Islami
Makkah Mukarramah

Reprinted in February, 2009
Printed in the U.S.A

Library of Congress Control Number: Pending
ISBN # 1-56316-162-1

DEDICATED TO:

Those Slaves, Men and Women
Who Accepted Islam
and Suffered for Their Faith

ZAID IBN HARITHA
KHABAB IBN AL-IRAT
ABU FUKAIHAH
BILAL, THE Abyssinian;
SUHAIB, The Roman;
SALMAN, The Persian

SUMAYYAH, Wife of YASSIR and mother of AMMAR
LUBAINAH
ZINNIRAH
NAHDIYAH
UMM ABIS

RADI ALLAHU TA'ALA ANHUM
(May Allah be pleased with them all)

They were freed, in body and spirit by Islam
and made Masters, Teachers and Guides of the Ummah.

INTERNATIONAL AWARD

CERTIFICATE OF DISTINCTION
Awarded by
The Government of Islamic Republic of Pakistan

to the authors for writing:
Six textbooks of Sirah
Our Prophet I, II
Mercy to Mankind I, II
Messenger of Allah, I, II

12 Rabi' 1404
18 December 1983

CONTENTS

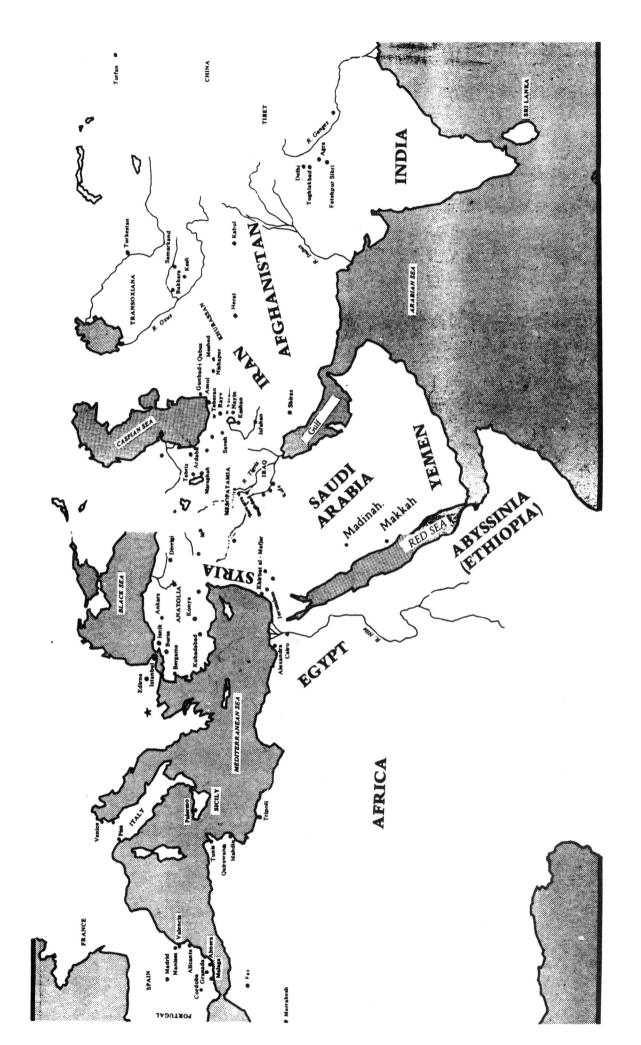

RECEPTION IN MADINAH

First Year Hijrah

It was a Friday. Rasulullah (S) started for Madinah. People in Madinah were waiting anxiously to receive him.

Rasulullah (S) and his party stopped at the outskirts of Madinah in the neighborhood of Bani Salim to perform *Jum'a* prayer. This was his first *Jum'a* in Madinah and he delivered his first Khutba (sermon). Some of the important points of his *Khutba* are:

> * I declare that Allah is One, and Muhammad is Allah's messenger whom He has blessed with guidance, light and wisdom.

> * The best advice a Muslim could give to his Muslim brother is to do good and be pious.

> * Your relationship to Allah should be based upon truth, sincerity, and obedience. This can best be achieved when you have no other personal motive in your life, but to please Allah alone.

> *Allah is truthful, He fulfills His promises, and He is full of mercy to His servants.

> *God has chosen you for Himself and named you Muslims (i.e., those who are completely obedient to Allah). Remember that the enemies of truth will be destroyed, but those who live with the understanding of the truth and on the strength of Allah's guidance will survive.

> * Allah alone is the Lord, and He alone has all power. Therefore keep your relations with Allah based on sincerity and piety, and work for the Hereafter.

The first *Khutba* in Madinah does not mention the atrocities of the *Kuffar* or his own suffering. It has no anger or venom. It invites humankind to Allah and speaks of His power. It also prophesies that the might of *Kuffar* will soon be broken, and Allah's help to His servants will make them victorious. Who else could believe this promise except those who had faith in the words of Rasulullah (S)?

BANU HARITH

TO NAJD

BANU ABD. AL-ASHHAL

BUHAIR

BANU MUAWIYAH

BANU AJABA

BANU ZAFAR

BANU QURAIZAH

BANU NAZIR

FADIH

FORT OF KA'B BIN ASHRAF

DITCH

WELLS

MASJID AL-NABI

BAQI CEMETERY

WELL

DATE GROVE

MOUNT UHUD

GRAVES OF SHUHADA

MOUNT SAL

JUMA

WELL

QUBA

HOUSE OF KULTHUM IBN AL-HADAM

MOUNT AIR

WELL

QIBLATAIN

TO SYRIA

DATE GROVE

WELL

DHUL HALIFAH

WELL

TO YAMBA

WELL

FORT OF SAID BIN ALAS

MOUNT HABASHAH

WINTER 81

The City Plan of Madinah at the time of Rasulullah(S)

ADAPTED FROM "NABI-I-REHMAT": SYYID A.H.A.NADWI

2

Rasulullah's party resumed their journey after prayer. Some people came to receive him outside the city. Others waited on the road to *Quba*. Litle girls and women stood in the way and on the rooftops to welcome their Prophet (S). They all sang a welcome song,

> The full moon has appeared
> From behind the Wada Mountain.
> We must thank God for this kindness.
> We must thank as much as we can.

The little girls of the tribe of Banu Najjar were pleased as they welcomed Rasulullah(S) into their neighborhood. This tribe is related to Rasulullah(S) on his mother's side. The girls sang together,

> We are the little girls of Banu Najjar.
> Muhammad, a beautiful neighbor you are!

Rasulullah (S) was pleased at this welcome. He had a special love for little children. He went over to the lovely children and asked them, "Do you love me?"

"Oh yes, *ya Rasulullah (S)*, we love you very much," all of them replied with joy.

"I love you too," Rasulullah (S) replied with a big smile.

In Madinah everyone wanted Rasulullah(S) to be his guest. It was very difficult for him to prefer one person over another. So he left the decision to his camel. "Wherever she stops," he told the people, "there I will stay."

Everyone watched the camel as she roamed. Finally she stopped in front of the house of Abu Ayyub al-Ansari. Abu Ayyub and his wife were overjoyed. Everyone felt the choice of Abu Ayyub al-Ansari's house had been made by Allah.

Abu Ayyub al-Ansari and his wife offered their house for Rasulullah (S) and his party and moved to the upper storey of the house. They were overjoyed to share whatever they had with their guests. Rasulullah(S) and some *Sahabah*(R) stayed on the first floor. This way the visitors who came to see him didn't disturb the family of the hosts.

In Madinah, behind the *Masjid al-Nabi*, the house of Abu Ayyub can still be seen.

Points of Review:

* Rasulullah (S) was warmly welcomed in Madinah.

* Everyone wanted to be Rasulullah's host.

* Abu Ayyub al-Ansari (R) was in fact chosen by Allah to be the host of Rasulullah (S).

Names to Remember:

Abu Ayyub al-Ansari   Banu Najjar   Banu Salem   Wada Mountain

Quranic Study:

1) The *Ansar's* support of the *Muhajirun* was worthy of merit. Read: *al-Nur* 24:22

2) The *Ansar's* sacrifice for the cause of Allah is aknowledged in the Quran. Read: *al-Hashr* 59:9 (We shall study more verses pertaining to the same subject later.)

3) By following Rasulullah(S), a Muslim becomes worthy of Allah's love: Read: *Ali Imran* 3:31

4) A Muslim is enjoined to follow Allah and His Prophet (S) as did the *Muhajirun* and the *Ansar*. Read: *al-Nisa'* 4:13, 69, 80; *al-Anfal* 8:1, 20, 46

Note the several other verses in the Quran that emphasize the obedience to Allah and Rasulullah(S).

NONE HAS THE RIGHT TO BE WORSHIPPED BUT ALLAH AND MUHAMMAD ID THE MESSENGER OF ALLAH.

LESSON 2

THE IMPORTANCE OF HIJRAH

Beginning of New Islamic Era

Hijrah, the migration of Rasulullah(S) from Makkah to Madinah, is a very important event in the history of Islam. The Islamic calendar starts with this event of *Hijrah*. All Muslims' must know its importance.

The departure from Makkah was not an unplanned and cowardly flight. It was under Allah's guidance. Rasulullah (S) had been preparing the ground for a long time. During thirteen years of life in Makkah, devoted *Sahabah*(R) were trained by Rasulullah (S)to help him in his future task of building a true Islamic life in Madinah.

Before the arrival of Rasulullah (S), most of the people of Madinah had already accepted Islam. Some Makkan *Sahabah*(R) of Rasulullah(S) had worked among the people of Madinah. Their work made the people of Madinah into *Ansar* helpers and supporters for the cause of Islam.

Rasulullah(S) had stayed in Makkah until almost all his *Sahabah*(R) had reached the safety of Madinah. He made his move only after he had received Allah's command to do so. He left behind his trusted cousin Ali to take care of the remaining work.

Thus, *Hijrah* was a well planned, divinely guided transition from the oppression of slavery to the freedom of Islamic life.[1]

Hijrah shows the complete submission of Muslims to Allah's will and Rasulullah's orders. When Allah asked the Muslims to leave their families, friends, homes, and country, they obeyed without hesitation. It was, no doubt, a big sacrifice on the part of the Makkan Muslims. That is why the Quran gives good tidings to *Muhajirun*,

---

[1]My father Mawlana Hamidul Ansari Ghazi, who read this chapter gave me a new insight into the meaning of Islamic *Hijrah*. He said,"Islamic concept of *Hijrah* is not a flight for safety or migration for better economic opportunity, but it is a divinely guided and well planned move from a point of weakness to a point of strength The purpose of *Hijrah* is to gain power and return to the point of weakness to make it a part of the center of strength.

Those who made *Hijrah* for the cause of Allah, after they were persecuted, we will surely give them goodly home in this world; and the reward of hereafter is even greater, if they would know it.

This was a great test of *Muhajirun's* faith and a great act of self-sacrifice. Through *Hijrah*, Allah taught us that when it comes to a choice between slavery and freedom, a Muslim must always choose freedom. If a Muslim is not allowed to practice Islam in a society, and he finds it impossible to change that society, he is required by Allah to leave that society and go to a land of freedom.

Those people who prefer temporary gains and security over *Hijrah* and continue to live a life of slavery are condemned by the Quran. At the time of death such compromise-makers will be asked by the angels why they chose that immoral un-Islamic life. They will have to answer that they were powerless and weak. The angels of death will then admonish them,

Was the earth of Allah not big enough for you to make *Hijrah* in it? For such people, their place will be Hell at the end of evil journey.

The *Sahabah*(R) of Rasulullah(S), however, were not among these weak-hearted people. They sincerely responded to Allah's call and made *Hijrah*.

Hijrah tells us about the Muslims' firm faith in the promises of Allah. Allah, on the night of *Mi raj*, had promised Rasulullah (S) that their trial was coming to an end. The power of *Kuffar* was going to break. The Muslims were going to be rewarded for their faith.

The Quran says in clear words,

And say: The truth has come, the falsehood was perished.
falsehood (by its nature) was bound to perish.
Isra' 17:81

A weak-minded person might have asked, "What kind of a promise is that?" The Muslims would have to leave their country and lose whatever they had. But no Muslim raised such a question. They felt honored to follow Allah's command. Their faith in His promise remained unshaken.

The Muslims knew that what Allah had for them in the future was best for them and that their true reward was in the Hereafter. They had no fear in their hearts about their future, and on their lips was the prayer which Allah taught them,

And O' Muslims, pray to Allah: "My Lord, make my entry by the gate of truth and make my exit through the gate of truth. And give me from your presence power to support me."

Isra' 17:80

Hijrah also shows the extreme love of the *Sahabah (R)* for Rasulullah (S). For *Sahabah (R)* the love for Rasulullah (S) was so great that life in Makkah would become meaningless without him. They were prepared to leave everything in order to be with him. In fact, no people in human history have shown such sincere dedication to their leader as did these early *Sahabah*(R) to Rasulullah (S). The Quran confirmed this love of *Sahabah*(R). "The Prophet is dearer to Muslims than their selves ..." *al-Ahzab 33:6*

Due to *Hijrah*, Muslims suffered many hardships, but they did not mind these physical discomforts. In *Hijrah* they saw the beginning of the fulfillment of the promises of Allah. Allah promised the *Muhajirun*,

Whoever makes *Hijrah* for the cause of Allah he finds much refuge and abundance in the world....

al-Nisa' 4:100

The *Muhajirun* believed in Allah's promise.

Soon the Muslims discovered that, although they had been a small minority in Makkah, in Madinah they were a majority. They had been disliked in Makkah; in Madinah they were welcomed. In Makkah they had not been allowed to say their prayers in public. In Makkah they left blood relatives and friends who were *Kuffar* in Madinah they found new brothers and sisters of faith who were Muslims. The life in Makkah had been a life of oppression and slavery; the life in Madinah was of political liberty and religious freedom.

Hijrah was thus the beginning of the fulfillment of Allah's promises. However, there were many more tests and trials ahead.

The Makkan Muslims who did *Hijrah* were called *Muhajirun*, the immigrants. The Muslims of Madinah who helped Rasulullah (S) and his Companions were called *Ansar*, the helpers.

Many other Muslims came from outside and settled in Madinah. All of them made the *Ummah*, "the Community", or "the Common Brotherhood" of Islam. Though strangers, they became friends and relatives. The Quran speaks about them in beautiful words,

And about the pioneers of Islam, first
of the *Muhajirun* and the *Ansar* - - -
And those who followed them in good deeds,
Allah is very pleased with them
And they are very pleased with Allah
al-Tawbah 9:100

This *Ummah* of Islam, which follows the *Sahabah (R)* in their good deeds, today consists of close to one billion people in the world. Its number has always continued to increase. It has never decreased.

Islam invites all mankind to forget their differences of race, language, color, and nationality, and unite in one *Ummah*, as did the Muslims in Madinah under the guidance of Rasulullah (S).

Points of Review:

* Islamic calendar starts with the events of *Hijrah*.

* The *Hijrah* was a well planned transition from slavery to freedom.

* The *Hijrah* shows Muslims' faith in Allah's promises and their love for Rasulullah (S).

Words to Remember:

Ansar, Hijrah, migration, *Muhajirun*, weak-minded

The Quranic Study

The Quran describes the *Hijrah* and the trials and rewards for the *Muhajirun* in many places. Study the following verses to have an understanding

al-Baqarah, 2:218; *ali-Imran*, 3:195; *al-Nisa'*, 4:97, 89; 100; *al-Anfal*, 8:72, 75;
al-Tawbah, 9:100; *al-Nahl* 16:41, 110
al-Tawbah, 9:100; *al-Nahl*, 16:41, 110; *al-Hashr*, 59:8

LESSON 3

CHALLENGES IN MADINAH

We know that human beings have many differences based on color, language, culture, religion, ideas, race, geographic origin, and political division. In human history whenever two or more such different people come to live together, it creates tensions among them and leads to wars and civil unrest. The strong always try to dominate the weak; one always enslaves the other. The love of their own color, tribe, race, and nation is so deep rooted in people that they automatically start hating, or even harming, those who are different from them.

In Madinah, Rasulullah (S) faced the task of making one *Ummah* or community from different tribes of Arabs, outside residents, Jews, and Christians. The task was so difficult that it could, in fact, be done only by a prophet. If mankind wants to get rid of its prejudice and unite in one *Ummah*, then it must follow the teachings of Islam and the example of Rasulullah (S). We shall, in this book, see what problems Rasulullah (S) had in building one *Ummah* in Madinah and how he solved them.

The people of Madinah were overjoyed. They had their Prophet(S) and their brothers in faith with them. It was a great honor. The *Muhajirun* were very happy also. They were with Rasulullah (S). They were living among their brothers in faith. They were free at last.

The *Muhajirun*, no doubt, missed their homes, friends, relatives, and, most important of all, their city. The difficulties of the new life of Madinah reminded them of the comforts they had left behind. But none of them complained when he remembered his home and the love of his relatives in Makkah. No one desired to go back. They looked forward to a new life in their new city. Madinah was their home from now on.

Rasulullah(S) however, faced many challenges in Madinah. Practical difficulties of making one *Ummah* of different groups and establish an Islamic State were formidable. First of all, there were problems within the Muslim *Ummah*.

There were two powerful Arab tribes in Madinah, Aws and Khazraj. They disliked each other. One would not accept the leadership of the other. They had

.fought many wars. The memory of the tribal war of Buath was still fresh in their minds. They were ready to fight each other again on any small pretext. Their enemies and the Jewish tribes in Madinah wanted them to continue to fight so that they would become weak and poor. Rasulullah (S) had to teach them to love and live with each other as good Muslims.

The *Muhajirun* from Makkah were mostly Quraish. But even among them were some people of other nationalities. For example, Bilal was from Abyssinia, and Suhaib was from Rome. There were also people from other Arab tribes who accepted Islam and lived in Makkah. These people were different from each other in many respects. But they had lived together as Muslims in Makkah under the training of Rasulullah (S). They had experienced the love which brotherhood in Islam creates in the heart of believers.

The *Muhajirun* and the *Ansar* not only belonged to different tribes, they had no experience of living together. The *Ansar* welcomed the *Muhajirun* but did they understand what it would mean for their own life. They had to share their meagre resources with the *Muhajirun*. In the future they were going to face war from the *Kuffar*. No one could say that they would still be brothers to each other after the initial welcoming period was over. One could easily fear the start of a civil war and the return of the days of *Jahilliyyah*.

Rasulullah(S) was sent by Allah to bring mankind together and to teach, even to the adversaries, the art of living together. Allah proclaimed the mission of Rasulullah (S), "And we have not sent you except the giver of good tiding and a warner for the entire mankind . . . ."*Saba* 34:28. This divine vision for Rasulullah's mission would have remained only an idea if he had not shown through his personal example how mankind could be united and taught to live together.

With the arrival of *Muhajirun*, Madinah became a city in which several nations lived. It was natural for them, as for all human beings, to compete with each other and fight with each other. But Rasulullah(S) personally taught them how to live together. The Muslims in Madinah have set an example for mankind to see how strangers and even former enemies could become brothers by believing in Islam. In fact, the world has no other example of this nature.

Some tensions in the world are due to economic reasons. The rich want to become richer and the poor resent it. In poor countries, people fight because there is not enough for them. In rich countries which have more than enough for everyone, people fight because of greed: they want to get even more out of life.

The *Muhajirun* and the *Ansar* were not rich. Some *Ansar* were relatively better off, but most of them were small farmers. Their lands were hardly enough for even their own needs. Many times they had to borrow from the Jews for their everyday needs. It is true, they had invited Rasulullah (S). But it was only after the arrival of the *Muhajirun* that they would know that it meant a lot of economic hardship for them. the *Muhajirun* had hardly anything with them. They had nothing to share with the *Ansar* except their good-will and faith. If the *Ansar's* faith wasn't firm, they were sure to resent these outsiders after a while.

Under the guidance of Rasulullah (S), the people of Madinah proved that indeed they were *Ansar*, the helpers of Allah. Their faith in Allah and love of Rasulullah (S) made them overcome all the problems. Unlike other people, instead of competing in becoming richer, the *Ansar* competed in self-sacrifice and in sharing their resources with the *Muhajirun*.

The *Muhajirun* were poor but not greedy. They did not come to Madinah for wordly motives. They were deeply touched by the love of their *Ansar* brothers. They were a grateful people. They were happy to be Muslims and to be *Muhajirun* in the way of Allah. They had a desire to serve Islam and not to share the wealth of their *Ansar* brothers. Thus, there was no tension. Instead, there was a lot of good-will on both sides.

What had happened in Madinah was, in fact, a miracle. The Muslims were fortunate to have Rasulullah (S) as their leader. He not only taught them to share their few things and care for each other, but he also set a noble example for them.

Thanks to the Islamic spirit and Rasulullah's teachings, the *Muhajirun* and *Ansar* established a harmonious community. The Quran rightly calls it a blessing of Allah,

> . . . .It is Allah who has helped you with His aid and the Company of believers. And moreover, He puts love between the hearts of believers. If you had spent all there is on earth you could have not succeeded to unite their hearts. But it is Allah who has united them in love. Indeed! Allah is Mighty and Wise.
>
> *al-Anfal 8:62-63*

The inner challenge to the unity of Muslims was much less serious than external challenges the *Ummah* faced. If the Muslim community's spiritual life had been weak and the Muslims' character not good, the outside challenges would have destroyed them. Rasulullah (S) spent all his time training the Muslims, teaching them Islam, and building their character. The *Ummah* faced many outside threats and challenges which wanted to destroy it.

Among people of Madinah there was a group of people who said they were Muslims. In fact, they were not Muslims. They were *Munafiqun*, hypocrites. With the Muslims, they behaved as Muslims, but secretly they supported the enemies of Islam. They thought they were in this way deceiving Rasulullah (S), but Rasulullah (S) knew about them through *Wahi*, revelation. He, however, showed extreme patience with them. Allah tells us about their deception,

> And among the people there are those who say, "We believe in Allah and the day of judgement." But, in fact, they are not Muslims. They think they deceive Allah and the believers, but they do not deceive any one except themselves, though they do not realize it.
>
> In their heart is a disease (of hypocrisy) and Allah increases their disease...
>
> *al-Baqarah,* 2:8,9,10.

The leader of the *Munafiqun* was Abdullah bin Ubai. He wanted to be the king of Madinah. With the arrival of Rasulullah (S) he lost his chance. He became an enemy of Rasulullah (S) and of Islam. Abdullah called himself a Muslim, but secretly he worked against Islam. Thus, the *Munafiqun* became inside informers for the enemies of Islam and a threat to the Muslim community.

In Madinah, there lived several tribes of the Jews. Three of them were prominent, *Qainuqah, Banu Nadhir,* and *Banu Quraidah.* They controlled the business. Many of them owned rich date orchards and farms. The Jews followed the teachings of Prophet Musa (S). They read *Tawra't* (Torah). *Tawra't* told about the coming of our Prophet(S). Rasulullah (S) had naturally thought they would welcome him. They were "the People of the Book." They believed in one God and Allah's revelations. They should be the natural allies of the Muslims against the idol worshippers of Makkah.

Rasulullah(S) wanted to live in peace with the Jews. The Jews, however, believed they were the chosen people of Allah. They disliked the Arabs. They thought that only they and not the Arabs could have a prophet. Learned Rabbis among them knew that Muhammad (S) was a prophet. A few of them accepted Islam and became a part of the Muslim *Ummah*. But most of them became jealous. They opposed Rasulullah(S), ridiculed him, and conspired against him.

Allah said in the Quran,

> Strongest in enmity — to the believers among the people you (O'Muhammad) will find the Jews and the non-believers . . .
>
> *al-Ma'idah* 5:82

Unlike the Christians whom the Quran calls closest to believers *(al-Ma'idah 5:8)* the Jews proved no better than the *Kuffar*.

There was also another reason why the Jews opposed Islam. The Jews were businessmen and money lenders. They loaned money to the needy *Ansar* at the highest interest. They cheated them in business and confiscated people's property unlawfully. The Quran condemns this practice strongly,

> That they took usury, though they were forbidden, and ate from peoples' wealth unlawfully, and we have prepared for the disbelievers a painful punishment.
>
> *al-Nisa* 4:161

As long as the people of Madinah were divided, the Jews continued to dominate them. But now that they were united and had Rasulullah (S) as their leader, the Jews could no longer make money by cheating the *Ansar*. Thus, for both racial and economic reasons, the Jews opposed Islam. We shall see how they first signed an agreement with Rasulullah (S) and then secretly started conspiracies against him.

The *Kuffar* of Makkah failed in their plans to kill Rasulullah (S), but their enmity to Islam remained firm. Although the Muslims had been forced to leave Makkah because of the oppression by the *Kuffar* the *Kuffar*, did not give up on them. The *Kuffar* had failed in their plans to stop Islam in Makkah, so they decided to destroy Islam and the Muslim *Ummah* in Makkah. They had seen how fast Islam was growing. "If Muhammad(S) is allowed to live," they feared, "he will destroy us."

The *Kuffar* knew that the people of Madinah did not like wars. The Makkans first tried to put pressure on the *Ansar* as they had done earlier with King Najashi to hand over Rasulullah(S) to them. The *Ansar* rejected this effort. The *Kuffar* then discussed plans to fight and defeat the Muslims. The Muslims were poor and still small in number. The *Kuffar* found willing allies among the *Munafiqun* and the Jews.

We should remember that in spite of the combined opposition of the *Kuffar* the Jews, and the *Munafiqun*. Rasulullah(S) did not have any one of them as his permanent enemy. He was sent as a mercy to mankind, and his effort was to bring all his enemies to the fold of Islam. Once any Jew, *Munafiq*, or *Kafir* accepted Islam, he became a part of the Muslim *Ummah*. We shall see how gradually Muslim *Ummah* grew from the ranks of its enemies.

In fact, Rasulullah's job in Madinah was much more difficult than it was in Makkah. But he was Allah's messenger, and Allah's guidance was with him. Besides, he had the most devoted followers. His *Sahabah (R)* were not the Arabs of *Jahilliyyah* who would fight for any reason. They were disciplined Muslims. They believed in Allah, loved their Prophet (S), and knew how to live together and help each other.

The Muslims were not like the followers of Musa(A), who demanded favors from Allah, but were not ready to make sacrifices. Nor were the Muslims like the disciples of Isa(A) who ran away leaving Isa(A) in the hands of his enemies.

Muslims were a patient and grateful people. They constantly thanked Allah for the favor of sending His *Rasul* among them and prayed to Him to enable them to serve Islam. They were eager to learn Islam and follow the *Sunnah* (tradition) of Rasulullah (S). They were ready to face every challenge. They knew that if they were firm in their faith, Allah's success and help would surely come.

For the next ten years, the Prophet (S) was busy in building a community, an *Ummah* of Islam in Madinah, while fighting his internal and external enemies.

Points of Review:

* Rasulullah(S) faced greater challenges in Madinah.

* The *Munafiqun* the Jews, and the *Kuffar* were united to defeat the Muslims.

* Muslims' faith was firm. They were united and ready to die for the cause of Islam.

Words to Remember:

Discipline   dominate   hypocrites   *Munafiqun*   *Sunnah*

Quaranic Study

1. Read *al-Imran*, 3:64. The Jews and the Christians are the People of the Book. See how Islam tries to establish a partnership of believers with them.

2. The Muslims should enter into dialogue with them in a most reasonable manner.

3. The Muslims are permitted to eat the food of *Ahl al-Kitab*. and the Muslim males can marry their women (*al-Ma'idah* 5:5).

4. Following verses describe different traits and attitudes of "the People of the Book." What do these verses say about them?
al-Baqarah, 2:109, 144, 146, 174 - 176.
ali-Imran, 19 - 23, 69 - 78, 98 - 101, 110 - 115, 119.

5. Study the following verses which portray the attitude of the *Munafiqun* to Islam and Allah's promise to punish the *Munafiqun*.
al-Baqarah, 2:8-20
al-Tawbah, 9:63 - 69; 73 - 78.

LESSON 4

FOUNDATION OF THE ISLAMIC COMMUNITY

First Year of Hijrah

Building of the *Masjid al-Nabi*
(The Mosque of The Prophet)

Establishment of *Muwakhat* (Brotherhood)

The first task of Rasulullah(S) in Madinah was to build a *Masjid* for the Muslims. Allah wants the Muslims to build a *Masjid* wherever they go. The Quran says,

> Indeed the *Masjid* of Allah will be built and visited by those who believe in Allah and the Last Day, establish *Salat* and pay regular *Zakat* and fear none except Allah . . . . .
> *al-Tawbah*, 9:18

Rasulullah(S) and His *Sahabah(R)* showed us the meaning of this verse.

In front of Abu Ayyub's house, there lay an empty plot of land. It was the property of two orphans. Rasulullah(S) purchased it from them.

Rasulullah (S) and his companions worked hard to build the *Masjid.* Everyone felt honored to work side by side with Rasulullah(S) for the building of the *Masjid.* People carried stones, mud bricks and pillars made of date trunks. As they worked they sang together,

> There is no comfort but the comfort of the hereafter,
> O' Allah! Have mercy on the *Ansar* and *Muhajirun.*

Rasulullah (S) himself worked harder than anybody else. *Sahabah* wanted him to rest and let them do the work. But he did not agree. He always did what he taught. For the cause of Allah he was not ready to do less than anyone else. His example shows us that for the leaders of the Muslim *Ummah*, it is important to work harder than other Muslims.

Rasulullah(S) advised us, "For anyone who builds a *Masjid* for Allah, Allah builds a house for him in Paradise."

TWO

VIEWS

OF

MASJID

AL-NABI

Seeing Rasulullah (S) work so hard, the *Sahabah* were encouraged. They instantly composed a couplet and sang it,

How can we rest when Rasulullah (S) works,
This act of ours will be the worst.

When the *Masjid* was completed, it was a very simple, square-shaped building, about fifty yards wide. It was made of mud, stones, date bark, and date leaves. There was a platform called *Suffah*. This became the house of those poor Muslims who had no homes. They are called *Ashab-al-Suffah*, the people of *Suffah*.

The people of *Suffah* had no means of their own. They had clothes which barely covered them. They had hardly any food to eat. For the love of Rasulullah (S), these people preferred to stay in the *Masjid*. Rasulullah (S) showed them special affection. He shared with them whatever little he had. These people spent their nights in prayer and days in learning Islam. This *Suffah* may be called the first residential university of Islam.

Soon after, a few small rooms were added to this *Masjid* for the family of Rasulullah (S). After some time, Sawda (R), the wife of Rasulullah (S) whom he married after Khadija's death, arrived to stay in these rooms. She was later joined by young A'isha (R) when she arrived from Makkah.

Rasulullah (S) himself led five daily prayers. Most of the time he was in the *Masjid* with other Muslims. The *Masjid al-Nabi* is the second holiest place of Islam.

The *Masjid* was many things to Muslims: a house of worship, a university of Islam, a meeting place, a government office, and a military headquarter. Rasulullah (S) showed that a *Masjid* must be the center of Muslims' total life. Through his example he showed us that before Muslims build their homes, they must build a *Masjid*.

Rasulullah (S) discussed with Muslims the method to inform people about their daily prayers. It was not until the second year of *Hijrah* that a *Sahabi*, Abdullah bin Zaid, had a dream; someone taught him the words of *Adhan*. Rasulullah (S) liked it. Umar (R) soon confirmed that he saw a similar dream. The words were accepted as a way to invite people to say their *Salat*. Bilal of Abyssinia (R) became the first *Mu'adhdhin*, "Caller of Prayer." Ever since, believers are called to *Salat* by these words five times a day.

An equally important task for Rasulullah(S) was to arrange for homes, food and money for the *Muhajirun*. They did not want to be a burden on their *Ansar* brothers.

One day the Prophet(S) called the *Muhajirun* and the *Ansar* together. He told the *Ansar* to accept the *Muhajirun* as their brothers. Each *Ansar* must accept a *Muhajir* as his brother. He said, "For Allah's sake two of you become brothers to each other." He himself held the hand of his cousin Ali and said, "This is my brother." People knew the love of Rasulullah(S) for Ali and Ali's love for Rasulullah(S). They understood Rasulullah(S) wants them to establish similar relationship of pure love and devotion for the sake of Allah alone.

Rasulullah's uncle Hamzah, the pure blooded Quraish, became the brother of Zaid, the freed salve of Rasulullah(S). Then one by one a *Muhajir* and an *Ansar* were picked by Rasulullah(S) and declared as brothers. This relationship is called *Muwakhat*, the brotherhood. They became like real brothers.

Each *Ansar* took his *Muhajir* brother home. He shared his house, land, and money with him. The *Muhajirun* were grateful. They accepted only as much as they needed. They became real brothers to the *Ansar*. Some *Muhajirun* soon learned farming. Others started business of their own. Some of them became very rich. They always remembered the kindness of the *Ansar* and helped their *Ansar* brothers in every way possible.

Points of Review:

* Rasulullah(S) built the *Masjid* as a center for the Muslims' total life.
* Rasulullah's own house was on one side of the *Masjid*.
* Rasulullah(S) invited *Muhajirun* and *Ansar* to establish *Muwakhat*.

Words to Remember:
Ashab al-Suffah, Masjid al-Nabi, **Mu**wakhat, *Mu'adhdhin*

Names to Remember:
Bilal of Abyssinia, Hamzah, Zaid

The Quranic Study

1. Compare the characteristics of those who established the *Masjid* in *al-Tawbah, 9:18* with those who destroyed it in *al-Baqarah, 2:114*

2. Read *al-Anfal, 8:72-75*. What do these verses say about *Muhajirun, Ansar,* and *Kuffar.*

LESSON 5

EVOLUTION OF THE ISLAMIC COMMUNITY

Rasulullah (S) was the leader of the Muslim *Ummah* in Madinah. The Muslim*Ummah* was going to be ruled by the Quranic laws and Rasulullah's commandments. The Jews of Madinah were not Muslims. They were not part of the Muslim *Ummah*. They had not accepted the authority of Rasulullah(S) as their ruler. It was not fair to impose upon them either Islamic law or Rasulullah's authority. Since now they lived in an Islamic state, it was important that a fair agreement be reached with them.

Rasulullah (S) wanted to be as just and fair to the Jews of Madinah as he was to the other citizens of the state. Rasululullah (S) talked to the leaders of the Jews. He said, "We live together in one city; therefore, we are one *Ummah*. We should live in peace and help each other. " The Jews accepted the idea and reached an agreement. Rasulullah (S) wanted the agreement to be written so everyone would know his obligation, and in case of a dis- agreement defined the rights and duties of both the Jews and Muslims. It was the first Written constitution of the world.

* Muslims and Jews are one *Ummah* (Community) of Madinah.
* Both will be free to have their own religion and law.
* Both will defend if either one of them is attacked.
* Both will make peace with outsiders together.
* Madinah will be a city of peace for both.
* All disputes will be decided by Rasulullah(S).

Rasulullah(S) thus showed that Muslims respect other people's religion. They also want to live in peace with their neighbors. In an Islamic state all non-Muslims have a right to their own religion and laws. They, like Muslims, have political rights and duties both in case of war and peace. An Islamic state, however, must be ruled by Islamic laws and Muslim head of government.

The agreement was signed but most of the Jews did not have any intention of accepting it. We shall see how they broke this agreement on many occasions and its effect on their relationship with the Muslims.

In the second year of *Hijrah*, Allah made *Sawm*, fasting, during the month of Ramadan an obligation. A *Wahi* told the Muslims,

> O believers! fasting is prescribed for you as it was prescribed for the people before you, that you may learn self-restraint.
>
> *al-Baqarah* 2:183

Sawm brings Muslims closer to Allah and other fellow human beings. Since a person fasts only for the sake of Allah, Allah Himself promises to be its reward. Fasting makes us experience hunger and thirst. We thus feel closer to those people in the world who are hungry and thirsty. It reminds us of the great bounties of Allah that we have and invites us to help the poor and the needy wherever they are.

Zakat, (regular charity) also became an obligation. The Muslims were asked to give a certain minimum portion of their wealth to the poor and the needy. The Quran said,

> Establish *Salat*, give *Zakat*, and lower your head in worship with those who bow their heads down in worship.
>
> *al-Baqarah*, 2:43

Zakat, however, is a minimum. Muslims are encouraged to give *Sadaqah*, charity, as much as possible. Allah promises a great reward for it. If *Sawm* made the Muslims realize other people's needs, *Zakat* made it an obligation for them to help other.

Muslims at that time prayed facing al-Quds (Jerusalem). Rasulullah(S) had asked the Muslims to turn to al-Quds. Because Kabah had become a temple of idols. Now Allah asked them to turn to Kabah, the first House of Allah. Now Muslims' faith had become deeply rooted. There was no fear of their turning to idols. Also, the time had come when Muslims should start thinking of cleaning the House of Allah from idols. Rasulullah(S) desired that Kabah be made a *Qiblah* (direction) for all the Muslims. *Wahi* told Rasulullah(S),

> We have seen the turning of your face for guidance to the Heaven, and now we have made you turn your face (in *Salat*) toward the *Qiblah* which is dear to you. So from now on turn your face toward the *Masjid al-Haram* (Kabah). And O Muslims wherever you may be turn your face in *Salat* toward it . . . .   *al-Baqarah* 2:144

The life of the Muslim *Ummah* thus was taking shape. Rasulullah's teaching and guidance, new *Wahi* from Allah, and mutual love of Muslims was making different people into one solid, united *Ummah*.

The *Munafiqun*, the *Kuffar* and the Jews, however, were not very happy.

Points of Review:

* Rasulullah(S) concluded a treaty of peace and friendship.
* *Wahi* made *Sawm* and *Zakat* an obligation.
* Makkah became the *Qiblah* of Muslims.

Words to Remember:

Agreement, Qiblah, Sadaqah, Sawm, Zakat

The Quranic Study

1. The Quran teaches us that the partners to a debt should write the agreement. This Quranic principle must apply to all understandings, agreements and contracts.
   Read *al-Baqarah*, 2:282-83 and write in your own words the basic rules the Quran is teaching in these verses.

2. Read *al-Baqarah*, 2:183-186. What do these verses teach about *Sawm* and *Ramadan?*

3. Read *al-Baqarah*, 2:142-150. These verses deal with the change of *Qiblah*. Understand the arguments of the Quran against those who objected to the change of *Qiblah*.

LESSON 6

JIHAD: A NEW POLICY BEGINS

Second Year of Hijrah

The Muslims loved peace. In Makkah they had been denied even the most basic human rights. There had been constant threats to their life and security. In Madinah they were finally with their Muslim brothers. They wanted peace badly. Rasulullah(S) needed time to devote to the urgent problems facing the Muslims in Madinah. He also needed peace to continue his *Da'wah* (preaching) among all the people. However, *kuffar* did not want to let Muslims live in peace and security. They feared if Rasulullah(S) was allowed time, the Muslim *Ummah* would become very strong. As the *Kuffar* were conspiring against the Muslims, they discovered that Jews were becoming hostile, too. They also found out that not all the Muslims were sincere. Some among the Muslims were *Munafiqun* who were showing open opposition to Islam.

The *Kuffar* found in Abdullah bin Ubai, the leader of the *Munafiqun*, a friend and an ally. They wrote to him, "If the people of Madinah will not stop helping Muhammad we shall attack them." Abdullah used this threat of the Makkans as an excuse to expel Rasulullah (S) and the *Muhajirun*. He approached the *Ansar* to seek their support in expelling Rasulullah (S). However, most of the people in Madinah were Muslims now. They had spent some time with Rasulullah (S). They loved him. They were ready to defend Rasulullah (S) and their *Muhajir* brothers from both the Makkans and the *Munafiqun*. The Muslims of Madinah became very angry with the *Munafiqun* and refused any help.

The *Kuffar* however continued their threats and conspiracies. Once Sa'd bin Ma'adh Ansari (R) visited Kabah. Abu Jahl, the arch enemy of Rasulullah (S), met him. Abu Jahl approached Sa'd bin Ma'adh (R) and told him with anger, "You have given refuge to these people who have given up their religion. Now you come to Makkah and expect us to protect you."

Sa'd bin Ma'adh was not scared. He replied to Abu Jahl, "We shall never give up Islam or our right to visit Kabah. If you stop us from worshipping in Kabah, we shall stop you from going to Syria for trade."

Some people then intervened and Sa'd was able to visit Kabah.

Muslims wanted peace, but the *Kuffar* would not allow them to live in peace even in Madinah. Muslims were forced to answer the Makkans on their own terms. Madinah lies on the way between Makkah and Syria. The caravans of the businessmen of Quraish passed through Madinah. The Muslims could now take revenge for the continued conspiracies of the Makkans. They decided to threaten the caravans of the Quraish. If the *Kuffar* hurt the Muslims physically, the Muslims could hurt the *Kuffar* economically.

Rasulullah(S) started sending parties of his Companions to watch the caravans of the Makkan *Kuffar* Once there was even a small fight between the party of Muslims and the *Kuffar* One *Kafir* was killed, two were arrested. The *Kuffar* captives, with their wealth, were brought before Rasulullah(S). It was a good revenge for the *Kuffar's* killing of Muslims and taking all their wealth. Rasulullah(S), however, did not like it. Allah had not yet permitted the Muslims to fight the *Kuffar* and kill them. Rasulullah(S) allowed these *Kuffar* to go home. He also returned all their wealth to them.

The *Kuffar*, instead of being grateful to Rasulullah(S), became more angry. They saw in the growing power of Islamic state a danger to their business and economic life. They started making preparation to attack Madinah and finish off all the Muslims before the Muslims became a serious threat.

Rasulullah (S) came to know about the conspiracies of the *Kuffar*. He made special security arrangements for the city of Madinah. Small security forces protected Madinah and kept a heavy round the clock watch. Rasulullah(S) sent out some parties to observe the movements of the *Kuffar*. He wanted to be on the safeguard from any surprise attack. He also make treaty relations with many Arab tribes around Madinah. These tribes were still *Kuffar*. Rasulullah(S) once again showed the peaceful intention of the Muslims.

Islam does not teach us hostility towards any people but to their wrong beliefs and practices. Rasulullah(S) had hoped that *Kuffar*, by being friendly to Muslims, could see the truth of Islam and become Muslims themselves.

Now Muslims were living in their own city-state. They faced constant threats from the outside and inside. Allah saw how patiently Muslims suffered for Islam. They had lived their faith without doubt. Allah granted them permission of *Jihad*, to struggle and retaliate against their enemies.

Jihad means to make an effort and to struggle in the way of Allah. This *Jihad* (struggle) one could do with one's money by giving it to the poor and for the cause of Islam. One can also do *Jihad* with one's effort by helping others and supporting justice and the right causes. One form of *Jihad* is to control oneself. It means not doing those things which are wrong, though one may feel even tempted to do them.

The most common meaning of *Jihad* is a war in the way of Allah to protect Islam and Muslims. It was this *Jihad* which Allah permitted the **Muslims**. *Wahi* told the Mulsims,

> The people (Muslims) against whom war is made
> are permitted to fight; because they were
> persecuted. In fact, Allah has the power to help
> them. These are the people who were expelled from
> their homes unjustly for saying our Lord is Allah. . . .
> *al-Hajj* 22:39-40

While the Quran allowed the Muslims to fight, it also set rules for *Jihad*. *Jihad* is not a war to kill and plunder. The purpose of *Jihad* is to defend justice and peace, and to oppose *kufr* and oppression. The force could only be used if it is essential.

It must also be understood that Islam does not allow Muslims to use force to convert people to Islam. The Quran says clearly, "There is no compulsion in religion." (al-Baqarah, 2:256). Allah wants people to accept Islam by their free will and not by force.

Islam's doctrine of *Jihad* shows that Allah permits the use of force when peaceful ways fail. When needed, force must be used for a just end; establishment of a just and peaceful society with equal rights for all. A peace which allows oppression, injustice, and exploitation to continue is immoral.

The Muslims were happy to receive the permission for *Jihad*. The time to suffer oppression helplessly was gone. Most Muslims were eager to die in the way of Allah and become a *Shahid* (Martyr). They knew that *Shuhada* (plural of *Shahid*) go to Paradise directly and are very dear to Allah.

Points of Review:

* The Muslims wanted to live in peace in Madinah but the *Kuffar*, the *Munafiqun* and the Jews did not want peace.

* Allah made *Jihad* an obligation in defense of justice and freedom of religion.

* *Jihad* means to make an effort and struggle in the way of Allah.

Words to Remember:

Caravan, *Da'wah*, economically, Human rights, *Jihad*

Names to Remember:

Abdullah bin Ubai

Quranic Study:

Jihad (struggle in the way of Allah) is often interpreted in the West as "Holy War" which Muslims must carry out to kill non-believers and to dominate the world. This is a fallacious notion. Abdullah Yusuf Ali describes the meaning of *Jihad* correctly.

> It (*Jihad*) may require fighting for God's cause, as a form of self-sacrifice. Its essence, however, consists in a true and sincere Faith, which so fixes its gaze upon God that all selfish and wordly motives seem paltry and fade away, and an earnest and ceaseless activity involving the sacrifice (if need be) of life, person and property in the service of God (takes root). Mere brutal fighting is opposed to the spirit of *Jihad*, while the sincere scholar's pen, or wealthy man's contributions may be the most valuable forms of *Jihad*.
>
> *The Holy Quran* n. 1270

Study the following verses to understand the spirit of *Jihad*.

al-Tawbah 9:20; *al-Hajj* 22:78; *al-Furqan* 25:52; *al-Ankabut* 29:69; *al-Saff* 61:10-14

LESSON 7

THE GHAZWAH OF BADR

The *Ummah* of Islam in Madinah was gradually taking shape. The Muslims were no longer at the mercy of the *Kuffar* but were masters of their own destiny. The *Kuffar* feared the rising power of the Muslim *Ummah*. Their special fears were for the safety of their trade route to Syria.

Once, a rich Makkan caravan was returning from Syria with large profits and valuable merchandise. They also bought war material to be used against the Muslims.

The caravan, as it approached Madinah, became fearful of a possible attack by the Muslims. The leader of the caravan, Abu Sufyan sent to the *Kuffar* of Makkah and asked for their help. The Makkans now realized the danger of the Muslim power in Madinah. They decided it was a good opportunity to crush the Muslims once and for all.

They started making war preparations. More than one thousand of the best fighters among the Makkans set out to fight a war with the Muslims in Madinah. They had seven hundred men in armor, seventy horses, a large number of swords, and enough supplies for all their people.

Rasulullah(S) ordered those who are ready to follow him in order to seize the rich Makkan caravan. It would be quite correct as the *Muhajirun* had left their houses and belongings to the Makkans. It would also provide many needed financial resources for the Muslim *Ummah*. Besides, it will be a fitting ans _ wer to the Makkan conspiracies and oppression. So not all the Muslims acc _ ompanied Rasulullah(S) in this *Ghazwah*.

When Rasulullah (S) and the Muslims were near Badr, they got the news that the caravan had escaped and that a big Makkan army was heading to_ wards Madinah. Rasulullah (S) stopped to discuss the new situation with the *Muhajirun* and the Ansar. He wanted to teach the Muslims that if they have

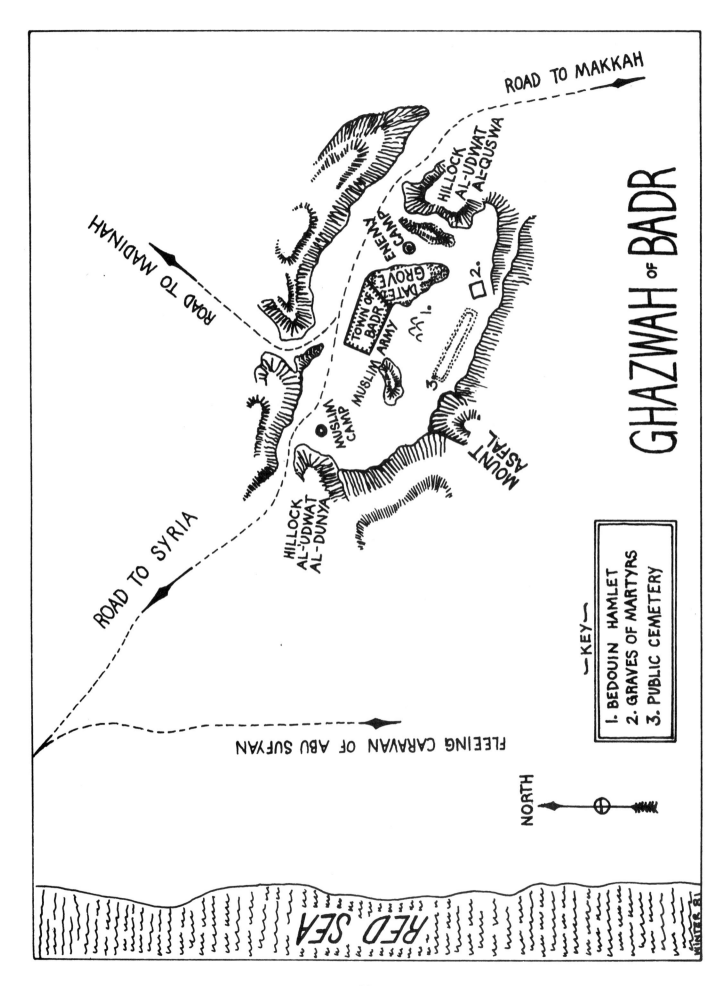

GHAZWAH of BADR

ROAD TO MAKKAH

ROAD TO MADINAH

HILLOCK AL-UDWAT AL-QUSWA

ENEMY CAMP

DATE GROVE

TOWN OF BADR

1.

MUSLIM ARMY

2.

3.

MUSLIM CAMP

ROAD TO SYRIA

HILLOCK AL-UDWAT AL-DUNYA

MOUNT ASFAL

─KEY─
1. BEDOUIN HAMLET
2. GRAVES OF MARTYRS
3. PUBLIC CEMETERY

FLEEING CARAVAN OF ABU SUFYAN

NORTH

RED SEA

MUNIR 81

28

faith, they will be victorious in spite of their small number. Some *Sahabah* (R)understood the intention of Rasulullah(S). Miqdad bin **Amr** (R), a *Muhajir*, said,

Ya! Rasulullah, wherever Allah has asked you to go there we shall follow you. We are not like the *Ummah* of Musa who left him and said, "We are seated here, you and your God can go and fight the enemies."

Abu Bakr(R), Umar(R) and other *Muhajirun* strongly supported the statement of Miqdad(R).

Rasulullah(S) then looked toward the *Ansar*. The support of the *Ansar* was most important in the war. They were the hosts. The *Ansar* had taken the *Bai'ah* (oath) to defend Rasulullah(S), but they did not have the *Bai'ah* to go out and fight the *Kuffar*. Now faith had more deeply entered the hearts of *Ansar*. As Rasulullah(S) looked toward their leader. Sa'd bin Ma'adh Ansari said,

"We believe in you. We shall obey you. You go ahead with your plans."

Other *Ansar* also promised their support to the Prophet (S). Rasulullah (S) was pleased with the faith of his followers. He decided to go on.

It was a very difficult decision to make. The number of Muslims was only three hundred thirteen. Their total war supplies consisted of three horses, sixty camels, and sixty suits of armor. They had a modest supply of food.

The *Kuffar* arrived at the valley of Badr early and occupied the high ground. The Muslim army found low and sandy ground. But the Muslims believed in Allah's help. They wanted to die fighting to become a *Shahid*, a Martyr to please Allah.

The armies of the Muslims and the *Kuffar* faced each other at the field of Badr. Badr is eighty miles south of Madinah. It was the first time the Muslims had a chance to cross swords with the *Kuffar*. At night, the Muslims slept well. They woke up fresh. There was some unexpected rain. It made the sandy ground firm and provided them enough water to make *Wudu* (ablution) and take a bath. It was, in fact, a divine help. Rasulullah(S) had spent most of his night in prayer.

In the morning, the armies faced each other. One thousand *Kuffar* against three hundred thirteen Muslims. The *Kuffar* were, naturally, very proud of their number and their war supplies. They were confident of victory. They did not know how strong Muslims' faith had made them.

The Muslims were sure of Allah's help. As the war was about to start, Rasulullah(S) picked up some dust, threw it toward the army of Kuffar, and said, 'Let the enemies faces be distroted."

Rasulullah (S) then turned to Allah for help. He raised his hands for prayer and said to Allah,

> O Allah, the Quraish are proud of their arms and their numbers. They have come to prove that Your Rasul is wrong. O, Allah, send help: The help which You promised. If the small number of Your faithful servants is killed, no one will remain to worship You and glorify Your name.

It was customary among the Arabs that before general war, a few soldiers from each side would meet in single combat. The Kuffar chose their best generals: Utbah, his brother Shaibah, and Utbah's son Walid. Three Ansar came forward to face them. Proud Quraish chiefs refused to fight the Ansar,"We are pure blooded Quraish. The Ansar are no match for us. Send us the right match so that we could prove our might."

Rasulullah(S) knew that this racial pride of Quraish would soon disappear. He pointed to Hamzah(R), Ali(R), and Ubaidah bin Harith(R). These brave soldiers came forward. There was an encounter, and the heads of Kuffar chiefs were soon lying on the ground in a pool of blood.

There were cries and wailings in the camp of the Kuffar and talk of revenge. The Kuffar soon realized that if these kinds of encounters continue they would lose all their brave fighters. Therefore, they declared a general war. A fierce battle then started. The small number of Muslims fell with full vigor on the Kuffar. They would either be victorious or become Shahid in the way of Allah. Allah saw the faith of the servants and sent an invisible army of angels to help the Muslims.

The Muslim youth attacked Abu Jahl, the worst enemy of Islam, and killed him. Many generals of the Kuffar started falling one by one. Soon they lost heart and ran helter skelter.

The Muslims fought bravely. They were helped by the angels. Seeing the angels, Makkans became scared and fled. As they ran, the Muslims picked up their arms and equipment. This is called *Mal al-Ghanimah* Among the Arabs it was the share of the victors.

Many of the famous leaders of *Kuffar* were killed. About seventy *Kuffar* were captured. Fourteen Muslims, six *Muhajirun*, and eight *Ansar* became *Shahid*, in the way of Allah. May Allah have His mercy upon them.

The captured *Kuffar* feared the worst from the Muslims. It was an Arab custom to kill all the enemies who were captured. Sometimes they were made slaves and were treated badly. The captured *Kuffar* were the worst enemies of the Muslims. They had killed innocent Muslims, expelled them from Makkah, and taken possession of their property.

Rasulullah(S) distributed the prisoners among the Muslims. He asked the Muslims to treat their prisoners kindly and not to take revenge upon them. Later they were allowed to pay for their freedom and leave. Among the prisoners were Abbas, an uncle of Rasulullah(S), and Abul As, the son-in-law of Rasulullah(S) and husband of Saiyyidah Zainab(R). They were treated like ordinary prisoners of war. No special concession was given to them.

Teaching the Muslim children was set as the price of freedom for the educated among the *Kuffar*. These prisoners had feared the worst, but they found Muslims were kind and fair. Some of them became Muslims and continued to stay in Madinah.

After the battle, the Quran prescribed special laws about the *Mal al-Ghanimah*.

Points of Review:

* At Badr, the first *Ghazwah* between the Muslims and the *Kuffar* took place.

* The small Muslim army won a big victory.

* Muslims treated the *Kuffar* prisoners kindly and freed them later.

Words to Remember:

Encounter, *Ghazwah*, Helter skelter, *Mal al-Ghanimah* To cross swords, *Wudu*

Names to Remember:

Abu Sufyan, Abu Jahl, Ali'Hamzah, Miqdad bin Amr, Ma'adh, Mu'awwidh, Shaibah, Sa'ad bin Ma'adh, Ubaidah bin Harith, Utbah, Walid

The Quranic Study

1.   *Sura al-Anfal* deals with the battle of Badr. It is an important *Surah.* You should read it carefully to understand the following points.

  i.   The decision to go to war was made by Allah (8:5-8).

  ii.   Allah's support was with the Muslims. 9:9-13, 43, 44, 64

  iii.   The struggle and sacrifice is important for the cause of Allah, 8:3, 15,16,39,72,74

  iv.   Compare the characteristics of the believers (8:2-4, 27, 45, 46, 63, 72) with those of the *Kuffar (8:13, 22, 30, 31, 34, 35, 36, 47, 49, 55, 56.*

  v.   See the rules about the *Mal al-Ghanimah,* 8:1, 41

LESSON 8

THE GHAZWAH OF BANI QAINUQA'

Our Prophet(S) had expected help from the Jews against the *Kuffar*. They were *Ahl al-Kitab*, the "People of the Book." That is why Rasulullah(S) called the Muslims and Jews of Madinah one *Ummah* (community) and signed an agreement of peace with them. Unfortunately, the Jews became hostile to Rasulullah(S). Their enmity to Islam went on increasing. In the battle of Badr, they openly sympathized with the *Kuffar* of Makkah.

The defeat of the Makkans made them sad. Some of them started openly inciting another attack of Makkans against the Muslims. The Jewish tribe of Bani Nadir had a great Arabic poet, Ka'b bin Ashraf. He wrote moving eulogies of the dead Makkans. He went to Makkah to incite the Makkans to a war of revenge and bloodshed against the Muslims. He wrote poetry to ridicule and laugh at Rasulullah(S) in order to please the enemies of Islam.

Among the Arabs, the poets had great influence over people. There was no radio, television, or newspapers. The poets controlled the minds and emotions of the people. Ka'b used all his power of poetry and his talent of speech against the Muslims.

He went to Makkah and recited his poems. Makkans heard these poems, remembered their dead, and took vows to fight the Muslims and finish them off. Ka'b reminded them of their past greatness as fighters and of their duty to destroy Rasulullah(S). Thus, through his poetry, he made sure that a big attack would be made by the Makkans to take revenge of the battle of Badr.

He also knew that as long as Rasulullah(S) was alive the Muslims morale would be high. So he tried to get Rasulullah(S) killed by a conspiracy. Fortunately, his conspiracy did not work.

Another tribe of Jews, the Bani Qainuqa, ignoring their agreement started teasing and harassing the Muslims. One day, a Jew undressed an *Ansari* woman in public and insulted her. When her husband learned of this, he was mad with anger. He killed the Jew. The dead Jew's friends and relatives killed the Muslim. This created a lot of tension between the Muslims and the Jews.

Our Prophet(S) wanted to settle the dispute by punishing the person who was responsible for this incident. The Jews did not agree. They told Rasulullah(S), "We are not the Makkans who ran away. We know how to fight."

As tension rose, the Prophet(S) sent an army to punish the tribe. They lived in fortified castles. Muslims surrounded their castles. The Jews now knew they could not win. So they asked for safe passage to leave Madinah.

At this time, no one would allow one's enemy to go unpunished. But Rasulullah(S) did not like bloodshed, so he allowed them to leave. That day, seven hundred Jews left Madinah for Syria. They were allowed to take with them whatever they could.

Other Jewish tribes continued to live as before. But these tribes became more bitter and hostile to the Muslims.

Points to Review:

* The Jews, instead of being friendly, became more hostile to the Muslims.

* Bani Qainuqa broke the agreement and started open enmity.

* There was a war which Bani Qainuqa lost. Rasulullah(S) allowed them to leave Madinah safely.

Words to Remember:
Ahl al-Kitab, Eulogy

Names to Remember:

Bani Qainuqa, Ka'b bin Ashraf

Quranic Study

We have seen the conciliating terms that Rasulullah(S) offered to the Jews of Madinah. The Quran also invited the *Ahl-al-Kitab* to unite for common purposes, but, unfortunately, the Jews did not reciprocate these gestures. The reasons for Jewish hostility lies in their general characteristics described in the Quran in detail. Read the following verses and see what reasons do these give for Jewish hostility.

34

1) *al-Baqarah* 2:40-86. The history of *Bani-Israel* (the Jews), the favors of Allah and their continuous disobedience.

2) *al-Baqarah* 2:80, 88, 90, 91; *al-Ma'idah* 5:18.

3) *al-Ma'idah* 5:14; *al-Anfal* 8:56

4) 5:42, 62, 53.

5) *ali-'Imran* 3:75, 181; *al-Ma'idah* 5:67.

6) *al-Nisa'* 4:155

7) *al-Baqarah* 2:19; al-A'raf 7:16

8) *al-Shu'ara'* 26:197

9) *al-Ma'idah* 5:82; *al-Baqarah* 2:75-79

LESSON 9

AN ISLAMIC MARRIAGE
Second Year of Hijrah

Rasulullah(S) had three sons and four daughters with Khadijah(R). His three sons were named Qasim(R), Tahir(R), and Tayyab(R)[1]. All of them died in infancy. His four daughters were Zainab(R), Ruqayyah(R), Ummi Kulthum(R), and Fatimah(R). Zainab(R) was married to Abu al-As. Ruqayyah(R) was married to Uthman bin Affan(R). Ruqayyah(R) died after her marriage. After her death, Uthman(R) married her sister, Ummi Kulthum(R).

Fatimah(R) was Rasulullah's youngest daughter. She was especially close to her father. Rasulullah(S) loved her very much. When the *Kuffar* used to mock and harm Rasulullah(S) in Makkah, little Fatimah(R) would comfort her father. She was only seven years old when Khadijah(R), her mother died. Fatimah(R), being the youngest child, felt the loss of her mother more than other sisters. Rasulullah(S) was very concerned about her and showed her special affection. After her mother's death, she became even more attached to her father.

Ali(R), Rasulullah's cousin, lived with him in Madinah. In the second year of *Hijrah*, Ali(R) was twenty-one years old. He was thinking of marriage, but he had neither money nor property for the marriage expenses. He liked Fatimah(R). Ali(R) was very close to Rasulullah(S); so was Fatimah(R). Ali(R) felt that marriage to Fatimah(R) would bring him even closer to Rasulullah(S). He decided to propose this marriage to Rasulullah(S).

Rasulullah(S) had a special love for Ali(R). Besides, there was no youth like him among the Muslims. He was handsome, brave, learned, and faithful. He was the first Muslim among the youth.

Arab fathers, at that time, had a right to marry their children to whomever they wanted. Islam teaches children to respect their parents and their parent's opinions in important matters of their life. Islam also recognizes the rights of the boys and girls to choose their partners. Islam taught the Muslims that parents must not marry their children without their children's consent as they did in the days of *Jahiliyyah*.

---

[1] Accounts differ on the number of male children of Rasulullah(S) from Khadijah(R). The number varies from one to three.

36

Rasulullah(S), therefore, wanted to know if Fatimah (R) would accept this proposal. So he went in the house and asked Fatimah's opinion of it. Fatimah(R) like other Muslim girls, was modest and bashful. She remained quiet. Feeling shy, she lowered her eyes and head. This was a quiet consent. Rasulullah(S) was very pleased by Fatimah's consent. He came out and congratulated Ali(R). This was the Islamic engagement.

Islamic *Shari'a* (law) asks the husband to pay a sum, *Mahr,* to his wife. This sum must be according to one's ability to pay. Rasulullah(R) asked Ali(R), "Have you any savings for the marriage?" He replied, "I have only one suit of armor and one horse. I can sell them and raise some money." Rasulullah(S) advised Ali, "A *Mujahid* (Warrior) needs his horse all the time. Go and sell the armor."

Ali(R) sold the suit of armor for four hundred eighty dirhams. It was a very small sum for a marriage. But Rasulullah(S) wanted to teach us that marriage should be simple.

Rasulullah(S) married Ali (R) to Fatimah(R) at the *Masjid al-Nabi* for a **Mahr** of four hundred eighty dirham. All the Muslims were happy. Everyone came to celebrate the marriage. Dates were distributed among the guests.

It is customary for parents to give some useful things to their daughters to be used in their new household. Rasulullah(S) gave Fatimah(R) a leather mattress, a water carrier, two millstones to grind flour, one ankle bracelet, and two earthen jars. Rasulullah(S) gave to his loving daughter the most he could give. It was an Islamic marriage; simple, dignified, and blessed. It was an example of an Islamic marriage for all time to come.

Ali (R) had no house. One of the *Ansar Sahaba* allowed the new couple to use one of his houses. Ali (R) moved there with Fatimah(R). Ali(R) and Fatimah(R) had a very happy marriage. They had three sons, Hasan(R), Husain(R) and Muhsin(R) and two daughters, Zainab(R) and Umm Kulthum(R).

Muhsin(R) died as a baby. Hasan(R) and Husain(R) were favored and loved by Rasulullah(S). He often played with them and allowed them to jump on his back and ride on his shoulders.

Fatimah(R) had no servants and did all the work herself. She fetched water, ground flour, cooked food, and took care of her children. She was pious and God-fearing. Rasulullah(S) called her "the leader of young women of Paradise."

Points of Review:

* Fatimah(R) was married to Ali(R) in a simple ceremony.

* Fatimah(R) had no servant and did all the work herself.

* Fatimah(R) and Ali(R) are the parents of Hasan(R) and Husain(R).

Words to Remember:

Ceremony, inviolable, *Mahr*, millstone, *Shara'a*

Names to Remember:

Fatimah, Hasan, Husain, Ruqayyah, Ummi Kulthum, Zainab

The Quranic Study

1. Study the verses about marriage in Islam and man-woman relation. *al-Baqarah*, "They (women) are your (men) garments, and you are their garments (2:187); *al-Nisa*, 4:1; *al-A'raf*, 189; *al-Rum*, 30:31

2. Polygamy is permitted but not recommended in Islam. Study the following verses to see the limited scope of polygamy. *al-Nisa'*, 4:3 129

3. Men and women are equal in the sight of Allah. The Quran refers and addresses to both of them in equal terms. See following verses: *Ali 'Imran* 3:195;

    But men have a degree of preference. See the reason. *al-Baqarah*, 2:228, *al-Nisa'*, 4:34.

38

LESSON 10

THE GHAZWAH OF UHUD
Third Year of Hijrah

It was the tradition of the Arabs to fight for revenge until either they succeeded or were destroyed. They believed their dead would be in discomfort if the living did not take their revenge. The Arab tribes were very proud of their nobility and bravery. Revenge was a question of honor. Because of their wealth and recognized nobility of birth, the Quraish of Makkah were even more proud of their ancestry than other tribes.

The defeat in the battle of Badr dealt a severe blow to their pride and prestige. The loss of their brave warriors made them extremely revengeful. They knew that with better preparation they could turn the tide of Islam back. So soon after the defeat of Badr, talk of war and revenge was heard in the streets of Makkah. Moving eulogies of the dead were written by the poets. We know the Jewish poet, Ka'b bin Ashraf, went to Makkah with a message of sympathy and support from Jewish tribes. The *Munafiqun* established a contact with the *Kuffar* to support them in any future war. Thus, big war preparations went on in Makkah.

Rasulullah(S) kept himself informed about the Makkan's preparation of war. He also knew of the conspiracies of the *Munafiqun* and of their Jewish allies in Madina. One day, he learned that an army of *Kuffar*, three thousand strong, had arrived near Madinah. They had started destroying the lands of the Muslims.

Rasulullah(S) invited all the Muslims to defend Madinah. He started with one thousand Muslims to face the *Kuffar*. But there were many *Munafiqun* among the Muslims.. In fact, the *Munafiqun* came with the Muslims to play a trick upon them. Their leader Abdullah bin Ubai, accompanied the Muslims for some distance. Then all of a sudden, he returned with three hundred of his followers to Madinah. He wanted to demoralize the Muslims by this trick. The Muslims were left alone to fight the *Kuffar*. However, the Muslims were not demoralized by this treachery of Abdullah bin Ubai. They had faith in Allah. They did not fear death. So they decided to go ahead.

Among the Muslims there were some people who were eager to fight in *Jihad*. They were not afraid of death. They, in fact, were eager to become *Shahid*.

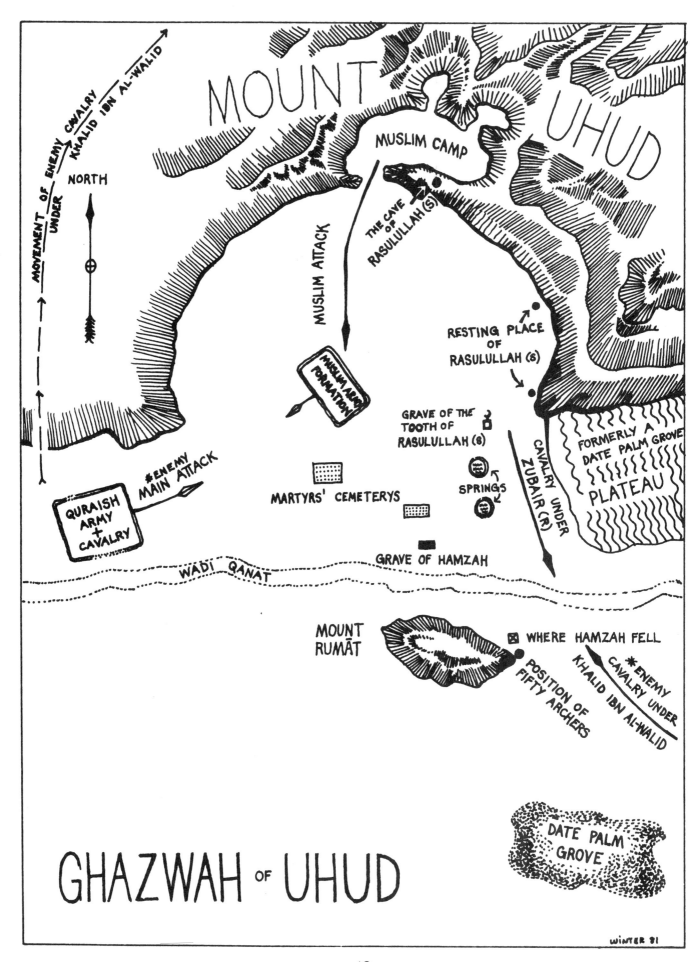

GHAZWAH OF UHUD

Among them were two children, Rafi' and Samrah. Rafi' stood on tiptoe to show Rasulullah(S) that he was an adult. Samrah was short. He was not accepted. Samrah told Rasulullah(S) that he was stronger than Rafi'. There was a wrestling match. Samrah defeated Rafi' to win his position in the Islamic army.

Rasulullah(S) and his companions were overjoyed to see the faith of the Muslim children. They said to themselves, "If our children are so brave, we should not care about the *Munafiquns'* treachery."

The Muslim army reached the field of Uhud first. They pitched their tents in front of the Uhud mountain. Rasulullah (S) gave everyone some task. Uhud mountain could safeguard Muslims from the rear. There was a big pass on one side. Rasulullah(S) appointed Abdullah bin Jubair and fifty archers to defend it. He told them, "Never leave the pass undefended"

The war started, and soon the army of the *Kuffar* was running away from the field. The Muslims chased them. Once again, seven hundred Muslims defeated three thousand *Kuffar*. They started collecting their *Mal-al-Ghanimah* (Booty). The archers who were guarding the pass saw the enemy defeated and fleeing. They wished to join other Muslims to get their share of the booty. Their leader, Abdullah bin Jubair, stopped them, but they thought the war was over. The pass was left with only their leader and a few guards.

The famous Makkah warrior, Khalid bin Walid, saw this opportunity. He collected a Makkan force and went around the mountain and came through this pass. The Muslims were surprised at this unexpected attack from the rear. They were scared and started running. Other *Kuffar* also returned to fight. Rasulullah(S) himself was hit by an arrow. He was injured. As blood flowed from his face, he raised his hands in prayer to Allah and said, "My Lord, guide my people to the right path of Islam, that they do not know."

The *Kuffar* made a concerted attack upon him. Arrows came from every side. Many companions tried to defend him and gave their lives saving him. Rasulullah(S), however, was neither fearful nor angered.

A rumour went out that Rasulullah(S) had been killed. Muslims were disheartened. Some felt so sad that they even gave up fighting. The Muslims defending Rasulullah(S) realized how this rumour was affecting the Muslims' morale. They announced, "Rasulullah is alive. He is still in the battlefield."

Muslims were overjoyed to hear the news. There was a new spirit. Once again they entered into battle and fought bravely. The army of the *Kuffar* left the field suddenly. They were tired and feared the new zeal of the Muslims. The Quran attributes the retreat of the *Kuffar* to a terror caused by Allah,

> Soon we shall create terror into the hearts of the *Kuffar*, for they associate with Allah other partners.

Ali'Imran, 3:151

Muslims suffered heavy losses. Seventy Muslims beccome *Shahid*. The Prophet's uncle, Hamzah, was killed. His body was cut up. His liver was chewed in revenge by a lady called Hind . Many Muslims were injured. Rasulullah (S) himself suffered many injuries.

Rasulullah(S) was still as full of confidence as ever. He asked Muslims to chase the *Kuffar*. Though seriously injured, he himself led Muslims to chase the *Kuffar* several miles. But the enemy was gone.

The Muslims returned to Madinah. They were sad for the loss of many dear friends. They also knew of their friends mistake in leaving the pass unguarded. But they were happy that Rasulullah(S) was safe.

There was a lady whose husband, son, and father had been killed. When she learned that Rasulullah(S) was safe, she thanked Allah and said, "If Rasulullah(S) is safe, I do not grieve for my husband, son, and father."

Some Muslims were angry with the *Munafiqun* and the Jews who had secretly supported the enemy. There were some Muslims who mistakenly followed the *Munafiqun*. They were now sad to have missed the chance to defend Islam.

The *Munafiqun* and Jews were happy at the losses of the Muslims. The *Munafiqun* told the Muslims, "If you had followed us you would be safe."

Allah made this battle a test for Muslims' faith.

Points of Review:

* An army of three thousand strong *Kuffar* attacked Madinah. The Jews and the *Munafiqun* secretly supported them.

* The Muslims first, won, but the Makkans attacked them through the pass.

* The Muslims suffered great losses, but their faith was not shaken.

Words to Remember:

Demoralize, eulogies, morale, tradition.

Names to Remember:

Abdullah bin Jubair, Abdullah bin Ubai, Hamzah, Khalid bin Walid, Rafi', Samrah

THE LESSONS OF UHUD

Fourth Year of Hijrah

At the battle of Uhud, Muslims were not defeated. But they did not win either. They suffered great losses. Many Muslims were killed and wounded.

After the miraculous victory of Badr, this was a great setback — if not a defeat. In fact, Allah had saved the Muslims through kindness after they were near destruction.

After the Muslims returned to Madinah, there was both discussion and soul searching for the people of Madinah. The *Munafiqun* who had deserted the Muslim army were happy that they made a wise decision. They went to the Muslims and told them, "If you had listened to us and followed us, you would not have seen such a day."

The Jews were pleased to see the Muslims humiliated. They could rightly give themselves credit for this humiliation. It was their poet, Ka'b bin Ashraf who incited the Makkans to war. The promise of support by the Jews was also responsible for the invasion of the *Kuffar*. The Jews and the *Munafiqun* were now thinking of completely annihilating the Muslims.

The reaction among the Muslims was, however, very different. First of all, they thanked Allah that Rasulullah(S) was saved. They knew that it was a test from Allah and that the purpose of it was to teach the Muslim *Ummah* a lesson as to how they should act in adversity and defeat.

The Muslims also analysed their weaknesses. It was disobedience to the commandment of Rasulullah(S) that had resulted in the Muslim losses. Muslims realized their mistake that instead of concentrating on the total annihilation of the power of the *Kuffar*, they had become busy collecting the *Mal-al-Ghanimah*.

There were Muslims who due to some weakness couldn't join the war. They were sincere Muslims, and they felt deeply disturbed by this loss. They felt it was partly due to their laziness and lack of responsibility that the Muslims had suffered. They had missed a great chance to serve Islam.

It was at this time that Allah sent his revelation to educate Muslims on the lesson of Uhud and to promise them future rewards.

There were those Muslims who were misled by the *Munafiqun*. They did not go to fight. Now they felt bad. They had missed an opportunity to fight for Islam and die in the way of Allah. They came to Rasulullah(S) and asked his and Allah's forgiveness. They were sincere, so Allah and Rasulullah(S) forgave them.

There were those good pious Muslims who went with Rasulullah(S) and fought in the battle. Some of them lost their relatives in the war. They were themselves injured. They were happy to be with Rasulullah(S) on the day of the battle. The *Wahi* told about such people,

> For those people who heard the call of Allah and His messenger after
> they were harmed in the battle; for such people who do good deeds
> and avoid evil deeds there is a great reward.
> *Ali 'Imran* 3:172

There were Muslim women whose husbands, brothers, and children were killed. They were sad for the loss, but they were patient. They were happy that their Prophet(S) was safe. They also knew everyone has to die one day. Allah chose their relatives to become *Shuhada'* in *Jihad* to honor them and reward them in the hereafter.

Allah told the Prophet(S) how happy their relatives were in paradise,

> Think not of those people who are slain in the way of Allah as
> dead; in fact, they are alive and receive their provisions in the
> presence of their Lord.
> *Ali 'Imran* 3:169

The Muslims also knew that those who left the pass unguarded were responsible for this tragedy. Allah told them in His revelation that obedience to Allah and His Prophet(S) is necessary for success. The Quran said, "Obey Allah and obey His messenger that you may find mercy." *Ali 'Imran* 3:132

Besides, victory and defeat are both from Allah. The Muslims will be victorious if they have faith in Allah and are patient in their defeat. A Muslim should never give up hope. The Quran warned, "If Allah is your helper none can overcome you; and if He withdraws His support who is there to help you? So let the believers put their trust in Allah," *Ali 'Imran* 3:160

Rasulullah(S) was neither bitter nor angry with this situation. He came to reform, teach and guide mankind. Both victory and defeat have an important message for Muslims. Rasulullah(S) knew the habits of the days of *Jahiliyyah* could not be changed so easily. The job of a Prophet is to remove the weaknesses of ignorance and give his followers a new moral life. He also knew that Allah, through this failure, wanted to teach Muslims some important lessons. This *Wahi* taught many important lessons to the Muslims, and Rasulullah(S) now spent his time in reinforcing the message of the *Wahi* and in rebuilding the character and morale of the community.

Although you may read the message in *Surah Ali-Imran*, 3:122-180, summarised below are the important points.

Muslims deserve Allah's help and mercy only if they obey Allah and His messenger.

True believers spend their money and exert their efforts in the way of Allah to please Allah. A true Muslim is kind, compassionate and, forgiving. He himself seeks forgiveness from Allah for all his sins and faults.

Allah has promised paradise for the believers. But the believers will pass through the tests and trials before they can enter paradise.

For the cause of Allah, many prophets and pious Muslims have sacrificed their lives. Death in the way of Allah leads to true and eternal life in Paradise. Every believer should aspire for that life.

It is only Allah who is eternal and who gives victory and defeat. The prophets are sent only as warners by Him. Muhammad(S) is a human, a messenger, like earlier messengers. He, too, one day will die. Therefore, the Muslims should look to the eternal message of Islam and not to the fact that Rasulullah was alive for their support.

Allah gave victory to the Muslims. Then they disputed and disobeyed, and Allah showed them the results of those disputes. Therefore, victory lies in faith, obedience and unity.

It is extreme kindness of Allah that He sent a messenger who is kind-hearted and of a loving nature to teach Islam and purify the bodies and souls of the believers. The believers should obey him in order to succeed.

As for the *Kuffar* the *Munafiqun*, and other enemies of Islam, Allah will destroy their power and give them painful punishment in the Hereafter. Allah will make the Muslims victorious, if they remain patient, fear Allah, and continue to have firm faith.

The Jews of Madinah had played an important role in the battle of Uhud. They were very happy at the suffering of the Muslims. Banu Nadir's poet, Ka'b, who had invited this attack, was killed by the Muslims. This made the people of *Banu Nadir* very angry with the Muslims. They broke their agreement with Rasulullah(S). They even secretly tried to kill Rasulullah(S) during the fighting in which they had openly sided with the *Kuffar*. The suffering of Muslims made them very bold, and they started showing open hostility towards the Muslims.

The Muslims were forced to fight the Jews once again. The Muslim army surrounded the Jewish castles. Facing the Muslims, the Jews locked up their forts and castles. For fifteen days the Muslims kept the siege. Finally, the Jews gave up on the condition that they be allowed to go safely. Rasulullah(S) allowed them to leave with everything that they could carry except their arms. They left with their camels, horses, and mules laden with their belongings. Many settled in Khaibar; others went to Syria.

The suffering of Muslims in Madinah encouraged Arab tribes to hurt Muslims more. Several of these tribes started harassing Muslims.

The people of *Adal* and *Qarah* invited ten Muslims to teach them about Islam. On their way, they killed eight of the Muslims and captured the other two. These two were sold in Makkah and were killed by *Kuffar* there. (Read their story in *The Stories of Sirah*.) The tribe of Kilab also invited Muslim teachers. Rasulullah(S) sent seventy of them. All of them except one were killed.

The Muslims were sad, but they were not disheartened. They knew Allah's help would surely come.

Points of Review:

* Through the suffering of Muslims in the battle of Uhud, Allah wanted to teach them some important lessons about victory and defeat, life and dealth, faith and patience.

* The Jewish tribe of *Banu Nadir* was expelled from Madinah because of its treachery.

* Some Arab tribes invited the Muslims to teach them Islam but killed many of them by trechery.

Words to Remember:

Siege, Treachery

Names to Remember:

Banu Nadir, Ka'b bin Ashraf, Khaibar, Kilab, *Adal, Qarah*

The Quranic Study

The reading of previous chapters will help you to understand Surah *Ali 'Imran* 3:122-180. Read this chapter and see what Allah says about the following. Give proper reference of the *Ayah's* in your answer.

1. How did Allah help the two weakhearted groups?

2. In what ways did Allah help the believers?

3. What should the Muslims do to become successful and victorious?

4. What will bring misfortune and defeat to the Muslims?

5. What did Allah promise to do to the *Kuffar*?

6. How does the Quran describe the character and role of Rasulullah(S) as a messenger of Allah?

7. What happens to the *Shuhada'*?

8. Were the promises made in these *Ayah's* fulfilled in the future?

LESSON 12

ALLAH GIVES A FORMULA FOR SUCCESS
Fourth Year of Hijrah

All evil habits are bad. Some of them destroy human beings both physically and mentally. They are bad for the individual and for society. According to the Quran four habits which are the worst enemies of human beings are: drinking, gambling, games of chance and idolatry.

Drinking is one of the vices which was as common among all the Arabs in the past as it is in our modern society. It is the root of all evils. By drinking, one loses control over one's mind and body. One has no control over one's actions. One endangers one's own life as well as the life of other human beings. Many other evil acts such as murders, rapes, and burglaries are committed by the drunk.

Islam teaches us that our mind is a special gift that Allah has given only to human beings. Allah wants us to use our minds properly. By the use of reason we can recognize Allah and His purpose in our life.

Drinking also destroys one's health. Alcoholism in itself is a sickness. In recent years, much research has been conducted into curing this sickness. Every bad habit is difficult to give up, but drinking is the worst. People who cannot stop drinking are alcoholics. These days, when alcoholics recognize their sickness and want to give up the habit, they have to go through special programs in clinics.

Gambling is another evil that is condemned by the Quran. Allah has given us a mind and body to use properly. Allah wants us to earn our living through honest work. Human civilization is built by hard work and not by gambling. Besides, in gambling many people lose their money while one takes it from them.

Gambling is also a kind of sickness. Compulsive gamblers do not stop when they win. They stake everything even when they start losing. History tells us, and we have everyday examples, that gamblers stake all their possessions, ignoring the rights of their families. Gamblers lose the habit of hard work and stop being a productive part of human society.

The Quran warns us about another human weakness, the desire to know about one's future. The Quran tells us that only Allah knows the future, and no one else has any knowledge of future events. Human beings are keen to know their future. They have invented methods like astrology, palmistry, and games of chance to determine future events. But these are only wild guesses, and superstition. People who use these methods have no faith, and are constantly worried about their future. They cannot act without consulting these fortune tellers. The fortune tellers take advantage of poor and ignorant people and give them false advice about which they don't know themselves, for a lot of money.

The time has come to tell the Muslims that faith in Allah alone and not in fortune tellers is essential for success in this life and in the Hereafter. Allah is kind and He always thinks the best for us. The Quran teaches Muslims to make an effort and then to rely upon Allah and accept whatever that effort produces. A Muslim should never worry about the future, but make an effort and leave the future in the hands of Allah. If we have faith, then we know whatever Allah does is best for us.

The Wahi came, it attacked the four major evils of Arab society and banished them forever. Allah spoke thus,

> O believers! Indeed, drinking (al-Khamr), gambling (al-Maisir), Idol worship (al-Ansab), and fortune telling (al-Azlam) are evil works of Shaitan. Leave them, in order that you may succeed.
> *al-Ma'idah 5:90*

Thus, in one stroke, Allah banned four evil things which were destroying Arab society. In fact, they destroy any human society. The Muslims had already given up idols. Now they gave up drinking, gambling, and games of chance. When this Wahi came, Rasulullah(S) sent a public announcer in Madinah. As soon as the people hear this they broke their cups, jars, and bars and repented to Allah. Some who were about to drink held their hand back and threw away both cup and wine. The wine was flowing in the streets of Madinah like water. When Umar(R) heard this announcement, he declared, "O Allah, we give these up forever."

Muslims are advised that in order to succeed in this world and in the Hereafter, they must give up these four evil things, al-Khamr, al-Maisir, al-Ansab, and al-Azlam, and place their trust in the hands of Allah.

Many societies have tried to ban these evils. They have even passed laws but have failed. The early muslims were so disciplined that they gave these things up immediately, and no good Muslim falls prey to these evils.

Points of Review:

* Drinking, gambling, fortune telling, and idolatry are the four major evils of human society.

* Muslims are told to give up these four evils in order to succeed.

* The early Muslims gave up these evils and Allah honored them with great success.

Words to Remember:

al-Ansab,al-Azlam, alcoholism, *al-Khamr, al-Maisir*, civilization, games of chance.

The Quranic Study

Drinking is an addictive habit. Allah prohibited it in stages. Read the following verses to see how gradual the order was.

al-Baqarah, 2:219; *al-Nisa',*4:43; *al-Ma'idah,* 5:90

LESSON 13

GHAZWAH OF AHZAB OR GHAZWAH OF KHANDAQ

(The Battle of the Ditch)

Fifth Year of Hijrah

For a long time it looked as if everyone was against the Muslims. The powerful Quraish, the Arab tribes, the *Munafiqun*, the Jews -- all were united and ready to destroy them. However, the Muslims were not scared. Rasulullah (S) had spent this time removing the weaknesses of the Muslims and building their character. Allah's *Wahi* told the Muslims what they must do to become successful.

The opponents of Islam knew they had a good opportunity to destroy the Muslims. They started uniting for a showdown. Some Jewish leaders from Khaibar went to Makkah and met the Makkan leader, Abu Sufyan. They wanted the Makkans to lead a final attack. Abu Sufyan agreed. These Jews then went to other tribes. The Quraish also sent their representatives to all the Arab tribes. All of them reached agreements and formed alliances (*Ahzab*).

The Makkans and their allies collected an army of twenty-four thousand[1]. The Quraish and the Jews were rich. They armed their men the best they could. "It is going to be the last war. There will not be any Muslims left after this," they thought.

Compared to this large army, the Muslims had only three thousand men. Rasulullah(S), as usual, discussed the war plans with the *Sahabah(R)*. Salman al-Farsi, a Muslim *Sahabi* from Persia, told the Prophet(S) a new method of defense. He told him that in Persia they dig a ditch (*Khandaq*) around the city. The enemy force cannot easily jump the ditch. The defenders fight only those who are able to cross the ditch. In this way, small numbers can defend the city against a powerful army. Rasulullah(S) liked the plan.

There were *Sahabah(R)* who wanted to go all out to fight the enemies and die in the way of Allah. But when Rasulullah(S) made the decision, everyone

---

[1]. According to some accounts the army was 10,000

accepted. An army of three thousand came out to dig a ditch in front of the city. A mountain protected them in the rear. Rasulullah(S) worked harder than any one of them. His example inspired the Muslims. The Muslims defended themselves from behind a ditch so it is called the Battle of the Ditch or *Ghazwah al-Khandaq.*

The Muslims were small in number. The *Munafiqun,* knowing the weakness of the Muslims, left. Rasulullah(S) decided to seek help from the Jews of Banu Quraida to come and help the Muslims according to their agreement. But they refused. In fact, they had a secret agreement with the *Kuffar* and were waiting for the defeat of the Muslims to join the armies of the *Kuffar.* When Rasulullah(S) heard this he said, "Allah is sufficient for us. He is our best friend."

The treachery of Banu Quraida made the city unsafe for women and children. The Prophet(S) had to leave five hundred Muslims to defend the city. Three thousand went to face the huge and powerful army of the enemies of Allah.

When *Kuffar* reached the ditch they were puzzled. They had not seen this kind of defense before. Many of them climbed over the ditch but Muslim soldiers took care of them. The *Kuffar* decided to wait, hoping that the Muslims would get tired and surrender. The Muslims were firm. The Muslim army continued to say their regular *Salat.* five times a day.

The Muslims were surrounded on three sides. They had no strength to attack the enemy and drive them away. Their supplies were running out. The *Munafiqun* enjoyed seeing the Muslims in this situation. They were hoping that in a few more days the battle would end with the complete destruction of the Muslims. One *Munafiq* sarcastically remarked, "Muhammad had been promised the treasures of *Kaiser* (Caesar) and *Kisra* (Khusraw) by Allah and look at the Muslims. They cannot go even to use the toilets."

The *Munafiq* was right about Rasulullah's promise and the serious situation of Muslims; but he did not know that Allah had decided to fulfil the promise of His *Rasul.* The response of the Muslims in this situation was just the opposite of *Munafiqun.* They were overjoyed to see the opportunity to serve Islam, and their faith increased. The Quran verifies their faith,

> When the believers saw the *Kuffar,* they said, "This is exactly what had Allah and His *Rasul* promised. Allah and His *Rasul* are true."
> This confrontation further confirmed them in their faith.
>
> *al-Ahzab,* 33:22

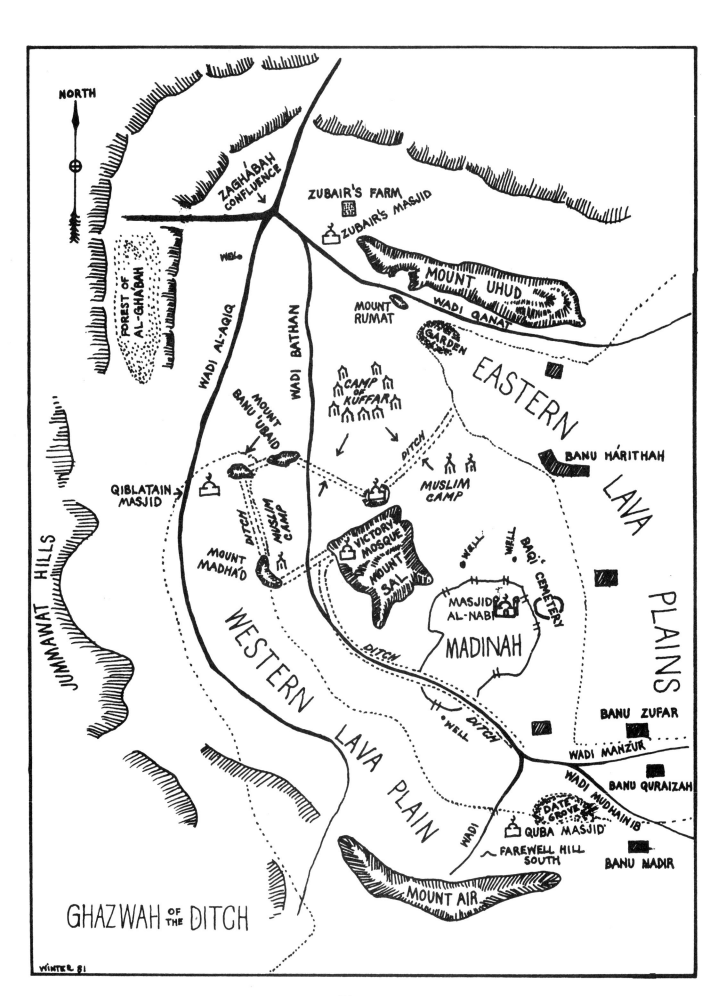

NORTH

FOREST OF AL-GHÁBAH

ZAGHÁBAH CONFLUENCE

ZUBAIR'S FARM

ZUBAIR'S MASJID

MOUNT UHUD

WADI QANAT

MOUNT RUMAT

WADI AL-AQIQ

WADI BATHAN

GARDEN

EASTERN

CAMP OF KUFFAR

MOUNT BANU UBAID

DITCH

BANU HÁRITHAH

QIBLATAIN MASJID

MUSLIM CAMP

LAVA

DITCH

MUSLIM CAMP

MOUNT MADHA'D

VICTORY MOSQUE

MOUNT SAL

WELL

WELL

BAQI' CEMETERY

JUMMAWAT HILLS

MASJID AL-NABI

MADINAH

PLAINS

DITCH

DITCH

WELL

BANU ZUFAR

WADI MANZUR

WESTERN LAVA PLAIN

WADI MUDHAINIB

BANU QURAIZAH

WADI

DATE GROVE

QUBA MASJID

FAREWELL HILL SOUTH

BANU NADIR

MOUNT AIR

GHAZWAH of the DITCH

WINTER 81

54

One day, the *Kuffar* made one big effort. Many *Kuffar* jumped the ditch. Some of them fell in the ditch and died. The Muslims fought bravely and killed or chased them. Ali (R) killed the most famous Arab Warrior, Amr bin Wudd. It was a hard day. On that day, several Muslims missed their *Asr* prayer.

Several days passed. The supplies of Muslims almost ran out. For several days they were on the point of starvation. Whatever little they had, they shared. In fact, there was not much left to share.

The *Kuffar* sent their spies to the Jews of Banu Quraida in Madinah. They wanted Banu Quraida to attack the city. The Jews of Banu Quraida were careful. Before they acted they wanted to make sure about the defeat of the Muslims. They also knew that Madinah was defended by five hundred brave Muslims. The Jews decided to send their spies to see the situation in Madinah.

One day, the Jews sent a spy to the women's quarters to find how well they were defended. Some Muslim women noticed the spy. Safya(R), an aunt of the Prophet(S), came out with a stick and hit the spy on the head. He died immediately. This incident created such a fear in the Jews that they decided to wait.

The situation was becoming worse but the Muslims were patient. One evening after a day's fight, Rasulullah(S) raised his hands and prayed to Allah,

> O Allah, You have revealed Your book. You swiftly take into account Your enemies. You defeat the enemies. O Allah, defeat them. Make them tremble with fear.

Allah had tested the faith of the Muslims. He heard the prayer of His *Rasul(S)*. That night, a fierce cold wind blew. It was so strong that it tore up the tents of the enemy. There was confusion. Some of their leaders started arguing and quarrelling among themselves.

The Jews were the first to leave. They went and stayed with their brothers Banu Quraida in Madina. They wanted to wait and see. They could join the war if the Muslims were defeated. But the Arabs also started leaving. One by one the Arab tribesmen left. Then the Quraish went away.

The *Kuffar* were defeated by a force which no one saw but which the Muslims knew. The Quran refers to this event and says,

> O believers, remember Allah's favor upon you when the enemy forces came to attack you. We sent against them fierce wind and an army that you did not see. *Surah*   33:9

This was a unique and unparalleled success; an example of successful war strategy, courage, vigilence, patience and faith. Every commander would be proud of his victory. Rasulullah(S), even on the day of such a great success, remained humble. He claimed no credit for the success. Instead, he raised his hand in thankfulness to Allah for *Dua* and prayed,

> There is no god but Allah,
> He is One,
> He made His army strong,
> Helped His servnt (Muhammad);
> He alone overpowered the enemy.

The Muslims returned to their homes with feeling of gratefulness to Allah(S) and His Prophet(S). But they felt very angry at the behaviour of their allies, the Jews of Banu Quraida. These people had broken their agreement two times earlier. They did it once again at a time of greatest peril for the Muslims of Madinah. Banu Quraida also gave refuge to the Jewish tribes who came to fight the Muslims. The Muslims thought if these people were allowed to stay in Madinah they would be a constant danger to the Muslims. The Muslims had asked the Jews for cooperation and peace. What they got in return were stabs in the back, conspiracies, and plots to kill their Prophet(S).

The Muslim army, after the victory of Khandaq, went straight to the castles of Banu Quraida. The Jews, as usual, locked themselves in. For several days they were surrounded. Finally, they agreed to surrender to Sa'd bin Ma'adh al-Ansari (R) instead of to Rasulullah(S). Rasulullah(S) agreed to the terms of the Jews.

Sa'd (R) asked the Jews how they wanted their affairs to be decided, according to Jewish law or Muslim law. The Jews said, according to the Jewish law. So Sa'd, according to Jewish law[1], decided that their warriors would be killed and their

---

[1]Deutronomy 20:13-14 describes the punishment for the cities which are far off thus:
> ...and when the Lord your God gives it into your hand you shall put all its males to the sword, but the women and the little ones, the cattle and everything else in the city, all its spoil, you shall take as booty for yourselves, and you shall enjoy the spoil for yourself, which the Lord your God has given you.

This punishment prescribed for the people of the distant cities, was given to the Jews. It was in fact a lenient punishment.

According to the Bible, the punishment which they deserved was,
> "...but in the cities of these people that the Lord your God has given you, you shall save nothing that breathes, but you shall utterly destroy them." See Deutronomy 20:16.

women and children be distributed among the Muslims. The Prophet(S) did not interfere with the decision of Sa'd(R). The Jews did not trust Rasulullah(S), and Allah did not want His *Rasul* to deal with them any more.

POINTS OF REVIEW:

* A large army of Makkans, Arab tribes, and Jews attacked Madinah, and Muslims defended themselves from behind a ditch.

* A fierce wind sent by Allah dispersed the *Kuffar* army.

* The Jews of Banu Quraida were punished for their treachery at a very difficult time.

Words to Remember:

Ahzab, Khandaq, sarcastic, showdown

Names to Remember:

Abu Sufyan, Banu Quraidah, Sa'd bin Ma'adh al Ansari, Salman al-Farsi

The Quranic Study

1. Read *Surah al-Ahzab,* 33:9-25. Note the reactions of i) the *Munafiqun,* ii) the *Kuffar* and iii) the Muslims in the war. How does Allah respond to the reactions of these groups?

2. Read verses 33:26-27. What punishment does Allah prescribe for the Banu Quraidah for their treachery?

3. Because of their disobedience the Jews were punished by Allah. Read *al-Baqarah* 2:61; *al-Ma'idah* 5:63; *al-I'raf* 7:, 166, 167, 168.

Lower level: *al-ʿazmat lillāh,* "Greatness belong to God".
Upper level, upside down: *aš-šukr lillāh,* "Thanks to God".

57

LESSON 14

THE TREATY OF HUDAIBIYAH
Sixth Year of Hijrah

Kabah was built by Prophet Ibrahim(A) and his son Prophet Ismail (A). It was the center of worship for all the Arabs. The Arabs stopped their wars during the four months of Hajj. No one could be prevented from worshipping there. To stop anyone from visiting Kabah was against the law of Arabia. But the *Kuffar* did not care about the law when it came to the Muslims.

After the victory of *Ghazwah* of *al-Ahzab*, Rasulullah(S) saw a dream; he was making *Tawaf* of Kabah with his followers. He saw in it an indication from Allah to perform *Umrah*.

In the month of *Dhul Qi'dah* in 6 A.H. Rasulullah(S) declared his intention to go to Makkah to perform *Umrah*. The Muslims were overjoyed. Fourteen hundred of them decided to go with him. The *Muhajirun* had not seen their homes or performed *Hajj* for the last six years. They were especially happy.

The love of one's country is natural among humans. The *Muhajirun* left Makkah in the way of Allah but they always missed it. Rasulullah(S) knew about their feelings. He always prayed to Allah, "O Allah, make the city of Madinah dear to us as you made Makkah dear to us — or even more so." The purpose of Rasulullah(S) was not to fight or to go to his home in Makkah but to perform *Umrah* and come back to Madinah. The Muslims took with them *Hadyi*, the animals for the sacrifice.

When the Makkans received the news, they started making war preparations. As Muslims approached Makkah, a few young *Kuffar* warriors came out to fight them. The Muslims had no intention of fighting. They arrested these people. They were presented to Rasulullah(S). He told them, "Our intention is only to perform *Umrah*. You can go and tell the Makkans."

The Quraish sent Arwah as their representative to talk to him. Rasulullah(S) told him, "The Muslims intend to do a peaceful *Umrah* for the sake of Allah. The Muslims do not want a war."

The Makkan representative saw the devotion and love of the Muslims for their Prophet(S). He went back and told the Quraish,

I have visited the courts of the emperors of Rome, Iran and Abyssenia. I found no one so popular among his subjects as Muhammad is among his followers. I have never seen a people more united and devoted than the Companions of Muhammad. If you fight with him, his friends will fight. They will die but they will never leave him.

He told the Makkans to allow the Muslims to perform *Umrah*. The Makkans were in no mood to permit the Muslims to enter Makkah. They continued their war preparations.

Rasulullah(S) then sent Uthman bin Affan(R), his son-in-law, to the Makkans. Uthman(R) was himself a Quraish. Because of his family ties he was respected by many of the Makkans. But the Makkans did not agree to the request.

Uthman(R) did not return for a long time. There was a rumor that the *Kuffar* killed him. Now Rasulullah(S) and the Muslims were very angry and wanted to punish the evildoers.

Rasulullah (S) sat under a tree and took the *Bai'ah* (oath) from the *Sahabah(R)*, to die fighting for Islam but not to turn their backs. This *Bai'ah* is called the *Bai'ah* of *al-Ridwan*. Allah had shown His pleasure for those who took this *Bai'ah*. The Muslims were now eager to fight.

After some time, the Muslims learned that Uthman(R) was safe. The *Kuffar* also learned that the Muslims were ready to fight. The People in Makkah knew very well that when the Muslims go to *Jihad* their aim is to become *Shahid*. The *Kuffar* had second thoughts. Now they wanted to prevent a war. They sent their representative to make a peace agreement with the Muslims.

The conditions presented by the Makkans did not favor the Muslims. Many Muslims did not like these terms. Rasulullah(S) wanted peace and he accepted them. These were the conditions:

* The Muslims should go back without *Umrah* this year.

* Next year they could perform *Umrah* and stay for **not** more than three days.
* If any Makkan becomes a Muslim and goes to Madinah, he must be returned.

* If a Muslim becomes a *Kafir* and comes to Makkah he will not be returned.

59

* Arab tribes will be free to have an agreement with either the Makkans or the Muslims.

* The agreement would last for ten years.

Many Muslims became unhappy with the treaty. The Muslims were strong and ready to fight. Their cause was just. "Why should we have this kind of treaty?" many of them objected.

The Prophet(S) said, "I am Rasulullah. I do what Allah asks me to do. Allah will help me in my decision." The Muslims then accepted his decision and obeyed him. Because the treaty was signed in Hudaibiyah, it is called the Treaty of Hudaibiyah.

Allah, in the Quran, called this treaty "A clear victory."[1] How could a treaty not favorable to the Muslims be called "a clear victory?" The Muslims believed in Allah and His *Rasul(S)*. They said Allah and His *Rasul (S)* know best. Only the future would tell how this treaty could prove a great victory.

The Muslims had fought for six years. They needed peace. Only in peace could everyone get to know the true nature of Islam.

As soon as Rasulullah(S) signed the agreement, a new Muslim convert, Abu Jandal(R), came running from Makkah. He was put in chains by the *Kuffar.* He told the Muslims how the *Kuffar* tortured him. The Makkans, according to the agreement, wanted him back. The condition of Abu Jandal(R) made the Muslims very sad. But Rasulullah(S) did not want to break his word.

The Prophet(S) told Abu Jandal(R), "Be patient. Have faith in Allah. Allah will find some way for you and other innocent Muslims. We have made the promise. Muslims do not go back on their word."

Abu Jandal (R) patiently accepted Rasulullah's decision. He went back with the *Kuffar.* Rasulullah(S) predicted that Abu Jandal(R) will lead an army against the Makkans. We shall later see how this prophecy was fulfilled.

Rasulullah(S) stayed three days in Hudaibiyah. The Muslims could not perform *Umrah*. The Prophet(S) asked them to sacrifice their animals and shave their heads to show their intention of *Umrah*.

The next year, the Muslims went to Makkah for *Umrah*. The Makkans left the city for three days in the care of the Muslims. The Muslims performed

[1] *al-Fath* 48:1

60

Umrah in peace and left after three days according to the agreement. Rasulullah's dream was thus made a reality by Allah. But that was not all. That was only the beginning of the great victory which the Quran predicted so clearly and forcefully.

Points of Review:

* The treaty of Hudaibiyah did not favor the Muslims but the Quran called it "a clear victory."

* Rasulullah(S) returned Abu Jandal (R) to the Makkans to honor his agreement.

* The Muslims came to perform *Umrah* the following year.

Words to Remember:

Bai'ah, prophecy, representative, treaty, *Umrah*

Names to Remember:

Abu Jandal(R), Arwah, Hudaibiyah, Uthman bin Affan(R)

LESSON 15

HUDAIBIYAH: A GREAT VICTORY

Rasulullah (S) and his party were on their way to Madinah when Rasulullah(S) received the *Surah,al-Fath*(The Victory). The Quran described the Treaty of Hudaibiyah "a clear victory." Revelation said, "Indeed We have given you a clear victory." *al-Fath*, 48:1. Many *Sahabah* (R) at that time did not understnad this description but they accepted it. They knew the decision of Allah and His *Rasul(S)* was best for them.

The Quran further promised,

> Truly, Allah has fulfilled the vision of His Prophet. You shall enter the *Masjid al-Haram*, if Allah wills, in peace, heads shaved, (or) hair cut short, and without any fear. For Allah knows what you do not know. And He granted before this a speedy victory.
>
> *al-Fath*, 48:27

The true meaning of "clear victory" and "Speedy Victory" would become known to the people soon. In fact, Islam is a religion of peace and always tries to avoid war. Other people can see the superiority of Islam only if they once meet Muslims, see them practice Islam, and learn about it from them.

Continuous war with the Makkans had not allowed other pagan Arab tribes to visit Madinah and meet the Muslims. The Makkans and their Jewish and *Munafiq* allies had the opportunity to go the other Arabs and spread false rumours about Rasulullah(S) and the Muslims. Now the Arab tribes and the Makkans had a chance to come to Madinah and visit the Prophet(S).

The Makkans and other Arabs started coming to Madinah. They saw the charming and loving personality of Rasulullah(S). They heard him recite the Quran. They spent some time in *Masjid al-Nabi* with other *Sahabah* (R). Many of them became Muslims. During the next one and a half years more Arabs accepted Islam than they did during the previous eighteen years.

It was at this time that Khalid bin Walid, the famous Makkan general (Remember that he attacked the Muslims through the pass at Uhud.) came to Rasulullah(S) and accepted Islam. Amr bin al-As, another famous Makkan general, also became a Muslim. Both, Khalid and Amr would be great generals and conquerors for Islam.

Now the Muslims understood the meaning of the Quranic revelation. There was another clear promise in the *Surah al-Fath* about the future of Islam. As the Muslims recited the verses, their faith grew stronger. They looked forward to the time about which the Quran spoke so forcefully and clearly.

> It is Allah who has sent His *Rasul* with guidance and the Religion of Truth to make His religion predominant over all religions. Allah is enough (for the believers) as a witness.
>
> *al-Fath*, 48:28

Points of Review:

* Islam is a religion of peace and always tries to avoid war.

* The Arab *Kuffar* came to Madinah, saw the Prophet (S) and the Muslims, and many accepted Islam.

* Khalid bin Walid and Amr bin al-As accepted Islam.

Names to Remember:

Amr bin al-As, Bai'ah al-Ridwan, Khalid bin Walid

The Quranic Study

Read the following verses of *Surah al-Fath.* Understand their teachings.

48:1-7 — about victory
48:8-9 — about the mission of Rasulullah(S)
48:10, 18-21 — about those who made *Bai'ah al-Ridwan*
48:25 — about one of the reasons for this agreement
48:27-28 — about promises of the future
48:29 — about the characteristics of Rasulullah(S) and *Sahabah (R)*

THIS IS BY THE GRACE OF MY LORD.

LESSON 16

ISLAM: A MESSAGE FOR MANKIND

Prophet Muhammad(S) was born in Arabia, but he was sent for all the people of the world. The Quran calls our Prophet(S) *"Rahmatun li al-Alamin"*, a mercy for all humanity. 31:107. Islam is a religion for all mankind. The Quran says, "Blessed is Allah Who has reveled the Quran to His servant Muhammad that he be a warner to all mankind. *al-Furqan* 25:1.

From the very beginning, there were many non-Arabs among the *Sahabah* of Rasulullah(S). But so far, Islam had reached mainly the Arab people. Now the time had come to take this message to everyone in the world.

Rasulullah(S) invited his *Sahabah(R)* and told them, "I am sent by Allah as a mercy to all mankind . Allah wants you to carry this message of Islam to the world. Be united and differ not among you as did the disciples of Isa (A)."

Rasulullah(S) dictated letters to the kings and rulers of Rome, Iran, Egypt, and Ethiopia and several other rulers and chiefs. The letters invited them to Islam. These rulers were mighty and powerful. At that time, Rasulullah(S) was no more than a chief of a small city-state. But he had the truth on his side. And one who has the truth is indeed most powerful. The texts of these letters came down to us from Muslim historians.

We can see in these letters the clarity of the message and firmness of faith. The letter to Caesar, Emperor of Rome reads,

> In the name of Allah the Mercy-giving, the Merciful. This letter is from Muhammad to Herculius, the Emperor of Rome.

> Blessed are the people who follow guidance. I invite you to accept Islam. If you do so you shall be saved and be secured. If you accept the fold of Islam, Allah will give you double the rewards. In case you refuse, then the burden of the sins of your people shall fall on your shoulders.

> O "People of the Book!" Come to the word that is common between us and between you that we shall worship none save Allah . . . .

Caesar, the Emperor of Rome received the letter of Rasulullah(S) in *al-Quds* where he was on a visit. He wanted to know about this Arab chief who could write such a frank letter to a powerful emperor. By chance, Abu

Sufyan, the leader of the Makkan *Kuffar*, was on a business trip in Jerusalem (al-Quds). The emperor invited him and talked to him.

Caesar: What is the family of this prophet like?

Abu Sufyan: It is a noble family.

Caesar: Are the people who accepted Islam weak or strong?

Abu Sufyan: Mostly they are weak.

Caesar: Are his followers increasing or decreasing?

Abu Sufyan: Increasing.

Caesar: Did he ever tell a lie?

Abu Sufyan: Never.

Caesar: Does he ever break his promise?

Abu Sufyan: Not so far. Now we have an agreement *(Hudaibiyah)*. We have to see if he stands by this agreement.

Caesar: What does he teach?

Abu Sufyan: He teaches,"Worship only one God.Don't accept any partners with Him. Offer *Salat*. Be pure in your life. Speak the truth. Be kind and considerate to each other."

Caesar was very impressed by Abu Sufyan's statement, especially since it came from someone who was an enemy of Islam. Caesar said, "It seems that Muhammad is a true prophet. If he is a true prophet, he might conquer even my empire. I wish I could visit him."

Caesar was Emperor of the biggest Christian empire. His ministers and clergy did not like his remarks. They silenced him. However, within twenty-five years most of his Eastern Empire was captured by the Muslims.

The Iranian Emperor, Khusraw Parvez, read the letter and became very angry. His empire spread as far as Yemen in South Arabia. He thought Muhammad(S) was his subject and under his authority. He tore up the letter and told the governor of Yemen, "Arrest this man Muhammad and present him to me."

The governor of Yemen sent two officers to arrest Rasulullah(S). When these officers came to him he said, "Your Emperor is already killed. Go back and tell

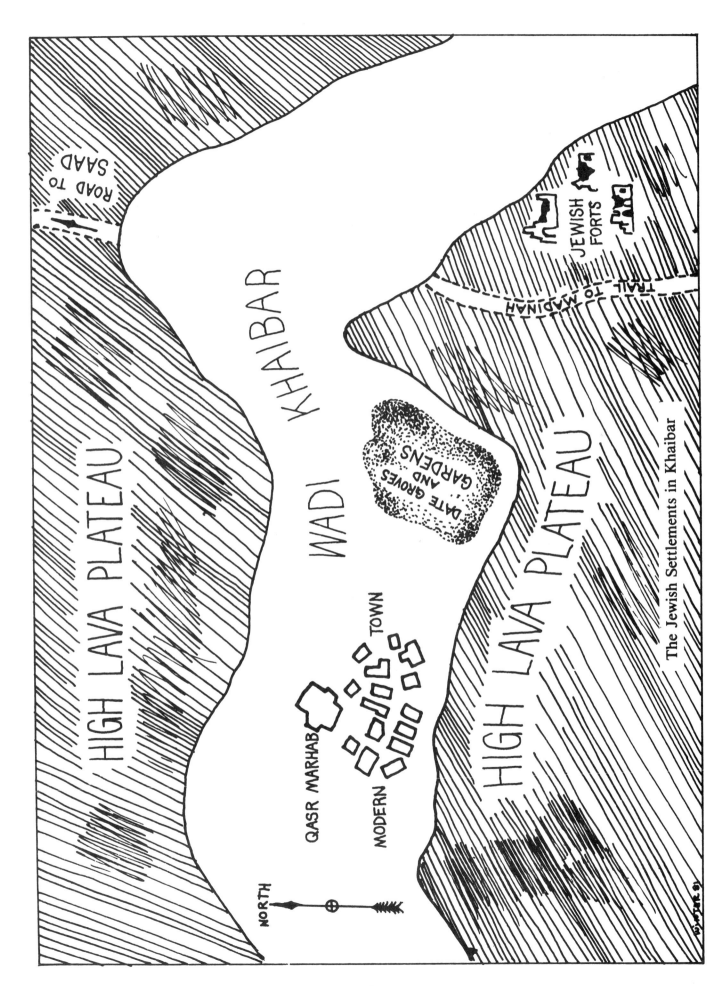

The Jewish Settlements in Khaibar

66

your governor that the Islamic state will reach the capital of your empire." The two officers later discovered that the emperor was killed by his son. At that time, no one could believe that within five years a small Muslim army would capture the capital of Iran.

The ruler of Ethiopia had already protected the Muslims and had become a Muslim. He said *Shahadah* once again. Other Ethiopian emperors remained Christian. But they had the blessings of Rasulullah (S) for their good treatment of the Muslims. The dynasty lasted until 1974 when the last emperor was overthrown. This emperor reversed the policy of his ancestors to protect Muslims. He killed the Muslims and expelled them from his country.

The Egyptian ruler did not accept Islam. But he received the Muslims kindly. He sent them back with many gifts. Prophet Muhammad's letter to the Egyptian ruler is still in the Topkapi Museum in Turkey. Egypt was conquered by Umar bin al-'As(R) seven years later.

Rasulullah(S) continued to send such letters and special missions to the people and tribes. Some ambassadors of Rasulullah (S) were killed by the *Kuffar* tribes or Christian rulers. After the conquest of Makkah the number of *Da'wah* (inviting to Islam) delegations and preachers sent by Rasulullah(S) increased considerably. In fact, after the peace of Hudaibiyah many tribes them- selves took the invitations and sent their delegation to Rasulullah(S) to accept Islam.

The Eastern Roman Empire (now called Turkey), Egypt, and Iran are now great Muslim nations. Each of them played an important role in the spread and expansion of Islam.

The defeat of the *Kuffar* and the end of Banu Quraida had excited the anger of the Jews in Khaibar. They started organizing their forces against the Muslims.

When Rasulullah(S) found out about this challenge, he decided to take the initiative and end the conspiracy. A Muslim army of sixteen hundred left Madinah for the first time to take a preventive action.

The Jews in Khaibar were well fortified. Their castles had twenty thousand well armed soldiers. For twenty days the Muslims kept the seige. There were several encounters. In one encounter Ali(R) killed the most renowned warrior of the Jews. The killing spread fear and panic in the ranks of the Jews.

They knew how hopeless their situation was. They had seen the end of Banu Quraida in Madinah. They decided to surrender to Rasulullah(S). Their leaders discussed the matter and Rasulullah(S) pardoned the Jews and allowed them to stay in Khaibar. He levied a tax on their land for the Muslim state of Madinah.

* Rasulullah(S) invited the emperors and kings of his time to Islam.

* Within a short time, these powerful empires were conquered by the Muslims.

* The Jews of Khaibar surrendered. They were pardoned and allowed to stay in Khaibar.

Words to Remember:

Caesar, Khaibar, Khusraw Parvez, Topkapi Museum

The Quranic Study

Many orientalists (Western scholars of Islam) maintain that the mission of Rasulullah(S) was only for the Arabs and Islam spread to non-Arabs as an accident. Read the following verses to see the universal character of Islam.

1. Allah is the Lord of all. *al-Baqarah,* :1; *al-Falaq,* 113 and *Surah al-Nas,* 114.

2. Muhammad's mission is for all mankind, *al-I'raf* 7:158; *al-Ra'd* 13:7; *al-Ambiya'* 21:107; *al-Ahzab* 33:40, 45, 46; *Saba* 34:28, *al-Fath* 48:8, 9

3. Islam as a universal religion. *Ali 'Imran* 3:19, 20, 83-87, *al-Maidah,* 5:3, *al-Shura* 42: 13-15; *al-Jathiyah,* 45:18, *al-Saff,* 61:9.

THERE IS NO GOD BUT YOU, GLORY BE TO YOU. VERILY! I WAS DOING WRONG TO MYSELF.

LESSON 17

THE LIBERATION OF MAKKAH

Eighth Year of *Hijrah*

The *Kuffar* soon found out how the agreement of Hudaibiyah was helping the Muslims. Some of them wanted to break it. After one and a half years, the *Kuffar* broke the agreement by attacking the tribe of Banu Khaza'a, which had a friendship treaty with the Muslims. The efforts of Rasulullah (S) to keep peace with the Makkans failed.

In fact, the time had come for the Muslims to take the initiative. Rasulullah(S) now started making preparations to liberate Makkah from the *Kuffar* and purify *Bait Allah* (Kabah) from the idols. Allah wanted the Kabah to be made once again a center for all Muslims. It was time for the fulfillment of Allah's promise to break the power of the *Kuffar* once and for all. When Rasulullah(S) told his intention to march on Makkah, the Muslims were overjoyed. Many other Muslim tribes also welcomed Rasulullah's message.

It was the biggest event in the short history of Islam. The helpless Muslims had been expelled from their homes seven years before. Now they were strong enough to challenge the *Kuffar* in their home country. This was the day which Allah had promised the Muslims in Makkah, at a time when they were persecuted and weak. The *Kuffar* had laughed then at such promises. They would not laugh any longer. The Muslims had believed in Allah's promises and had prayed for this day.

Led by Rasulullah(S) on the tenth of Ramadan, in the eighth year of *Hijrah*, a Muslim army of ten thousand marched on Makkah. This was an army which was fasting for the sake of Allah. On their way they offered regular *Salat*. Many Muslim tribes joined as the army marched toward Makkah. On the way to Makkah, Rasulullah (S) saw his uncle, Abbas, coming from Makkah. Abbas had always been kind to Rasulullah(S) but he had not accepted Islam. Now he was coming to Madinah to become a Muslim. Rasulullah(S) was very pleased to accept Abbas to the fold of Islam. Abbas(R) become a soldier in the Muslim army.

When the Makkans heard the news, their leader Abu Sufyan himself and another *Kafir* Budail went out to confirm the news . He saw the army from a hiding

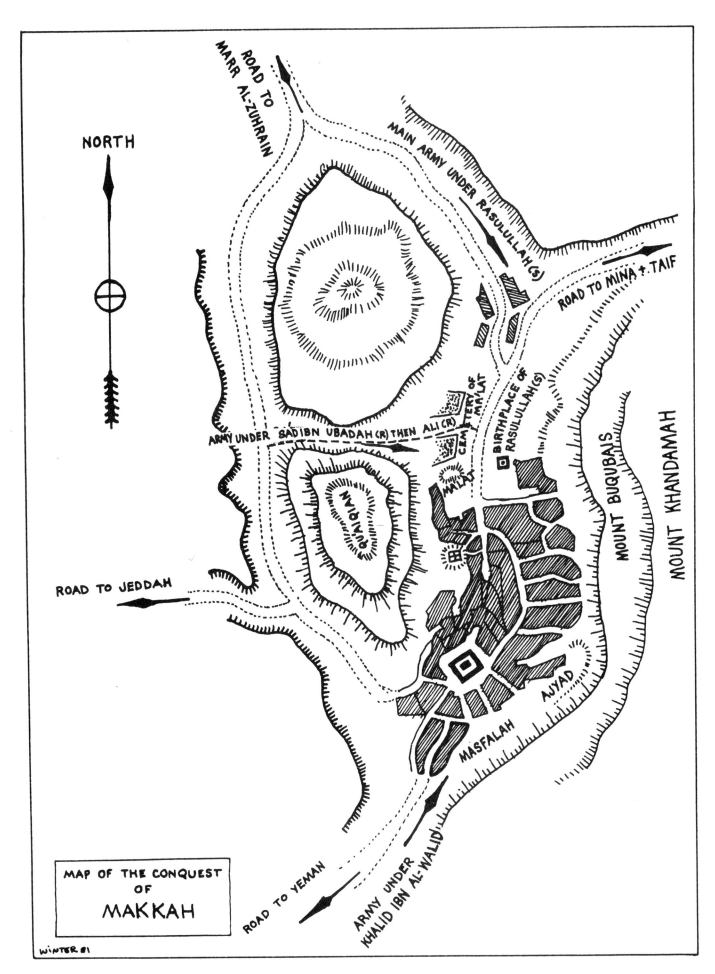

NORTH

ROAD TO
MARR AL-ZUHRAIN

MAIN ARMY UNDER RASULULLAH (S)

ROAD TO MINA + TAIF

ARMY UNDER SAD IBN UBADAH (R) THEN ALI (R)

CEMETERY OF MA'LAT

BIRTHPLACE OF RASULULLAH (S)

MA'LAT

QUAIQIAN

MOUNT BUQUBAIS

MOUNT KHANDAMAH

ROAD TO JEDDAH

AJYAD

MASFALAH

ROAD TO YEMAN

ARMY UNDER KHALID IBN AL-WALID

MAP OF THE CONQUEST
OF
MAKKAH

WINTER 81

70

place. Abbas(R) the newly converted uncle of Rasulullah(S), spotted them and arrested them. They were presented to Rasulullah(S). Abu Sufyan was the leader of the Makkan enemies. He opposed the Muslims, conspired to kill Rasulullah(S) and led military attacks on Madinah.

Any other ruler would have killed such an enemy but it was the court of Prophet of peace. Rasulullah(S) looked at both of them with affection and said, "Go in peace. You are free. Today there is no revenge. Allah is very kind."

Abu Sufyan and Budail were so moved by these words that they immediately became Muslims. Abu Sufyan (R) and Budail (R) are now remembered as devoted *Sahabah* of the Prophet(S). Rasulullah(S) then made a general declaration of amnesty (forgiveness) for all who wanted peace.

He sent Abu Sufyan(R) as an ambassador of peace to the Makkans. The Makkans lost heart when they learned that their leader was now a humble follower of Muhammad(S). Abu Sufyan(R) declared a message of peace on behalf of Rasulullah(S):

> There is peace for those who enter the house of Abu Sufyan.
> There is peace for those who enter *Bait Allah.*
> There is peace for those who stay in their own homes.
> There is peace for those who do not carry arms.

Only six enemies of Islam and killers of Muslims were not pardoned.

Rasulullah(S) instructed his army as they were ready to enter Makkah to be peaceful, to respect old people, women, and children.

Rasulullah(S) appointed Khalid bin Walid (R) commander of half of the army. He asked him to enter Makkah from one side. He himself led the other half of the army and entered Makkah from the other side.

Points of Review:

* The *Kuffar* broke the agreement of Hudaibiyah.
* The Muslims liberated Makkah.
* Rasulullah(S) pardoned the *Kuffar* of Makkah.

Words to Remember:
Amnesty, pardon

Names to Remember:
Abbas, Abu Sufyan, Banu Khaza'a Khalid bin Walid

LESSON 18

THE PURIFICATION OF KABAH

Rasulullah(S) and his army of followers did not come to seek revenge. They came to teach the message of Islam. Rasulullah(S) was a messenger of Allah, a mercy to all, teaching Allah's Oneness and inviting all mankind to live in peace and brotherhood. As the Muslim army advanced, their swords were in their cases. *Allahu Akbar* was on their lips.

Rasulullah(S) was mounting a camel, his head held low in humility before Allah. He recited the Quran, "Indeed, We (Allah) have given you a clear victory."

The Makkans were surprised to hear Muhammad's declaration of peace. They were even more surprised to see a conquering army entering their city with so much humility, showing no pride and seeking no revenge.

Rasulullah(S) and his Companions entered Kabah. Rasulullah(S) had a stick in his hand by which he hit the idols one by one saying, "The truth *(Haqq)* has come, the falsehood *(Batil)* has gone. The falsehood is supposed to go." The three hundred and sixty idols were removed and broken into pieces. The idols from inside the Kabah were thrown out. Then all the Muslims said *Salat* of thanks to Allah at *Maqam Ibrahim* (the Place of Ibrahim).

Once the fear of conquering Muslims was removed, many Makkans entered Kabah to see the Muslims. Among them were those who had fought the Muslims and killed many of their brothers in faith. They had expelled the Muslims from their homes and taken over their property. The *Kuffar* waiterd anxiously, wondering what Rasulullah(S) would do to them next.

Rasulullah(S) stood up and spoke to the crowd, saying:
There is no god but Allah. No one shares His power. He fulfilled His promise. He helped His servant Muhammad.

O people of Quraish, Allah has done away with the evil practices of *Jahiliyyah* (the days of ignorance). The pride in one's family is now gone forever. All human beings are brothers to each other. They are children of Adam. And Adam was made of clay.

From now on no one should take revenge for the blood of one's relatives. People must learn to live in peace.

Rasulullah(S) then recited a verse from the Quran,

O mankind, We have created you from male and female and created you in tribes and nations, so that you may know each other. The best amongst you is he who is most righteous.

He declared,

Allah and His messenger have forbidden drinking.

Then he looked at the Makkans, his face glowing with kindness instead of anger and asked them, "What do you think I am going to do to you?" The Makkans said, "You are our noble brother and son of our noble brother, Abdullah."

"Go in peace, no one will question you today," Rasulullah(S) told them. "You are free."

Rasulullah(S) told the *Muhajirun*, "Forgive your Makkan brothers. Do not demand your properties back from them.."

As the time of *Salat* approached, Bilal of Abyssinia (R) climbed up the roof of Kabah and said *Adhan*, "Alllahu Akbar, Allahu Akbar...."

Some *Ansar* had feared that Rasulullah(S) now might like to stay in his city, Makkah. They felt sad at this thought. Allah informed him of the *Ansar's* feelings. Rasulullah(S) told them, "I am a servant of Allah. I migrated to Madinah at His command. I promised to stay with you. I shall always live with you and die with you."

The *Ansar* were very happy to hear this. All the Makkan *Muhajirun* decided to follow the footsteps of their Prophet(S). They loved him so much. They could hardly remain without him.

The Prophet(S), who taught the Muslims to remain patient when persecuted, now showed them to be generous and kind at the hours of their greatest victory:

History has no other example of this kindness and generosity and faithfulness.

Points of Review:

* Rasulullah(S) cleansed Kabah of idols.
* He declared the evil practices of *Jahiliyya* ended.
* Most *Kuffar* accepted Islam.

Words to Remember:

humility, *Jahilliyyah*

Names to Remember:

Maqam Ibrahim

The Quranic Study

1. Read *al-Hujurat*, 49:13. See the basis of preference in Islam.

2. To understand the characteristics of Muslims, which secured them success read: *Surah al-Asr.* What are the four characteristics that are essential for success in the life and in the hereafter.

3. Rasulullah(S) said, "Allah has fulfilled His promise to His servant." The Quran has these firm promises of success for the believers spelled out in many places. Whenever you read the Quran, note specially these promises and see how Allah fulfilled them. You may, as an example, look to the following verses.

    al-Nur, 24:55-57
    al-Fath, 48:1-3, 20, 21, 27, 28

The names of the Seven Sleepers around that of their dog Qiṭmīr

74

LESSON 19

THE GHAZWAH OF HUNAIN

Eighth Year of *Hijrah*

Hawazin and Thaqif were two powerful and brave Arab tribes. They had opposed Islam vigorously. The news of the liberation of Makkah made them very unhappy. They would not allow the Muslims to control the Kabah, the house of their idols. They decided to make a last big effort against Islam. They were determined to destroy Islam or themselves.

The news came to Rasulullah(S) about gathering of a strong army by these Arab tribes, to attack Makkah. He decided to challenge the enemies before they were fully ready. So he marched from Makkah toward the tribes and met them in Hunain.

The army of the enemy was four thousand strong. The enemies brought their families and the cattle to the battlefront in order to fight to death.

The Muslim army was twelve thousand strong. It was also quite well armed this time. The Muslims felt happy to see their number and arms. Many of them forgot that it was not their number or arms, but Allah's help that brought them victories.

The valley of Hunain was surrounded by mountains. The road went through a narrow pass. The enemy archers hid themselves in the mountain pass. In the morning when the Muslim army entered the pass to go to the valley, the enemy showered them with arrows. This unexpected attack made the Muslims very nervous. Many of them, not knowing what to do, fled in every direction.

Rasulullah(S) stood on an isolated hill. The enemy spotted him and directed their full attack toward him. He stood there, fearless and full of confidence. From the hill he called to his Companions,

Come back.
I am Rasulullah.
I am not a false prophet.
I am the grandson of Abd al-Muttalib.

His uncle, Abbas(R) who had a loud voice, repeated Rasulullah's call. The Sahabah(R) heard this call. Their hearts were overjoyed to hear Rasulullah's call to them. They had realized their mistake. In response to Rasulullah's call, they answered, "Labbaika (we respond to you) Ya Rasulullah."

The Muslims had realized their mistake of relying on their numbers instead of Allah's power. They returned and threw themselves into the battle with new zeal. Now the tide turned in their favor. A fierce battle started. Soon the *Kuffar* tribesmen were fleeing. The Muslims chased them and arrested them. Six thousand prisoners were taken. A big *Mal-al Ghanimah* fell into the hands of the Muslims. The Muslims now fully realized that victory and defeat were not because of their numbers but by Allah's permission. Allah through a *Wahi* reminded them of this favor of Allah,

> Surely Allah gave you victory on many fields as well as on the day of Hunain, when your number elated you it did not help you. The land in spite of its vastness straightened you. Then you turned away in retreat.
>
> Thereafter, Allah sent down *Sakinah*, His peace and assurance, upon His messenger and upon the believers and He sent down the hosts of angel you did not see and punished the *Kuffar*.
> al-Tawbah, 9:25-26

Some *Kuffar* fled to Ta'if and took refuge in a fort there. The Muslim army advanced and laid a siege on the fort of Ta'if. After one month, Rasulullah(S) lifted the siege and prayed to Allah for the people of Ta'if to accept Islam. Allah accepted the prayers of His Prophet and a year later the people of Ta'if became Muslims.

Rasulullah(S) distributed the wealth and prisoners according to Islamic law. Soon the poeple of various *Kuffar* tribes which belonged to Bani Sa'd (the tribe of Halimah(R), the prophet's nurse) approached him for his forgiveness. He remembered the kindness of his foster mother and other foster relatives and willingly left his share and freed the prisoners. When the *Sahabah(R)* learned this, they followed Rasulullah's *Sunnah* and did the same. The Arab tribesmen saw Rasulullah's generosity and the *Sahabah's* love for their Prophet(S). Most of them became Muslims and became the devoted *Sahabah(R)* of Rasulullah.

Rasulullah(S) returned to Madinah with his *Sahabah(R)*. Some people of Madinah had feared that after the conquest of Makkah Rasulullah(S) and the *Muhajirun* would not return to Madinah but Rasulullah told them,

> If people would go through a valley and
> the *Ansar* go through another valley, I
> would go through the valley of the *Ansar*.

The Ansar were moved by the words of Rasulullah(S). Some of them even wept. After the great victory of Makkah and Hunain, he returned to Madinah.

Now Rasulullah(S) was the undisputed religious and political leader of almost all of Arabia.

Points of Review:

* In the battle of Hunain, the Muslims became proud of their large numbers; they were defeated by the enemy.

* Rasulullah(S) called the fleeing Muslims to come back; a Muslim victory followed.

* Prisoners of war and booty fell to the Muslims but soon the prisoners were released and the booty returned.

Words to Remember:

Foster-mother, undisputed

Names to Remember:

Bani Sa'd, Halimah, Hawazin, Thaqif.

VERILY! ALLAH PROVIDES SUSTENANCE TO WHOM HE WILLS WITHOUT ANY ACCOUNT OR MEASURE.

THE CHALLENGE OF THE ROMAN EMPIRE
Eighth and Ninth Year of *Hijrah*

The letters of Rasulullah(S) to the Roman Emperor brought him to the attention of the powerful Roman Empire. This empire was far too big and far too powerful to be concerned about Rasulullah's power.

The empire had many Arab Christian rulers as its clients and allies. Rasulullah(S) had sent his *Sahabah(R)* to invite them to Islam also. Shurjil, the ruler of Basra, killed the *Sahabi*, Harith bin Amir(R), who brought him Rasulullah's letter. In the eight year of *Hijrah*, Rasulullah(S) sent a force of three thousand soldiers to punish this ruler. At the head of the army was Zaid(R), the freed slave of Rasulullah(S). Next to him in order were Jafar(R), a cousin of Rasulullah(S), Abdullah bin Rawaha(R), a prominent Ansari, and Khalid bin Walid(R), the famous Quraish general. It was beneath the dignity of a high born Arab to be led by a former slave but Islam had now changed the whole outlook of the Muslims. Everyone obeyed Rasulullah(S), though there were still some people who did not like this choice.

Shurjil organized an army of one hundred thousand. The emperor sent another one hundred thousand soldiers to support Shurjil.

At the field of Mu'tah, three thousand Muslims met the powerful army of the Romans. Zaid(R), Jafar(R) and Rawahah(R) died one by one leading the Muslim army. Then Khalid bin Walid(R) took the command of the army. Khalid(R) was a brilliant general. The Muslims were full of faith and zeal. They knew that their small numbers made victory almost impossible for them. They could have returned to Madinah but they decided to fight. For a Muslim who goes to *Jihad* to become a *Shahid* to please Allah, there is no turning back.

As the war continued, the Muslims were surprised to see their resistance. Soon the Roman army retreated, perhaps to recuperate. Khalid bin Walid then gathered the remaining Muslim force and returned to Madinah. In Madinah Rasulullah(S) received the *Wahi* that informed him about the battle situation.

Rasulullah(S) told *Sahabah(R)* about the death of his cousin, whom he loved dearly, and other Muslims and the victory of Muslims through the *Saif Allah*, the sword of Allah, as he described Khalid. From now on, Khalid's title became *Saif Allah*.

The Roman Empire now realized the danger of the Muslim state's power. The Christian clergy also realized that Islam had become a great challenge to their Christian religion. The Christians believed in the Trinity of Father, Son, and Holy Spirit. Mariam was revered as the mother of Isa (A). They regarded Isa (A) as the Son of God.

Islam brought the message of Allah in its final form. It refuted Christian doctrines. It abolished the priestly class and established man's direct relationship with God. It gave all human beings, kings and common people, equal rights before the laws of *Shari'ah.* So both the priests and the kings became Islam's enemy.

After the battle of **Mu'tah**, Arab Kings and *Amirs* approached the emperor to face the rising power of Islam. The emperor asked his army generals to prepare for an assault on Madinah.

On his return from Makkah, Rasulullah(S) learned about the Roman war preparations. He had hardly rested from one campaign when he faced a greater challenge. Once again, he decided to face the enemy in his territory.

To challenge the Roman Empire was no joke. It was the biggest power of its time. Besides, the route to the north was rough through dry sand and rocky mountains and the weather was hot. The chances of a Muslim victory against such a powerful enemy were almost nil. Rasulullah(S) was in the sixty-second year of his life.

This campaign became the biggest test of Muslims' faith. All the Muslims, old and young, weak and strong, rich and poor were asked to enlist in the army and donate their money, arms, cattle, and horses to Rasulullah(S).

The Muslims knew the heavy odds against which they were working. But no questions were raised and no excuses offered. There was a general enthusiasm to find an opportunity to walk with Rasulullah(S) once again.

The *Munafiqun*, fearing the Romans, offered all kinds of excuses. They even tried to convince the Muslims not to take risks in the hot weather. Allah told them, ".... Say to them, hell fire is hotter than this, if they would understand...." *al-Tawbah* 9:81. The *Munafiqun* were sure that the outcome would be a big defeat for the Muslims.

There were also some weak-minded Muslims. Under the influence of the *Munafiqun* or out of sheer laziness, they excused themselves from joining the Muslim army.

Since all the allies of the *Munafiqun* (the *Kuffar* of Makkah and the Jews of Madinah) were defeated, they needed a plot against the Muslims carefully. For this purpose, they built another mosque near Quba. They met there to plot against the Muslims while the Muslims thought they were there to say *Salat* prayer. Allah exposed their conspiracies and called it *Masjid Dirar* (mosque to harm Islam). These *Munafiqun* approached Rasulullah(S) to lead *Salat* in that *Masjid* before he left for the campaign. Rasulullah(S) knew very well the nature of the conspiracy of the *Munafiqun* and so he excused himself from it then but promised that after his return he would look into the matter.

There were thirty thousand Muslim soldiers who started for Syria to face the Roman army. It was the biggest army that Rasulullah(S) had assembled. But it was no match for the hundreds of thousands of Roman soldiers. Besides, the Romans had a professional army. The Roman soldiers were paid by the emperor; the Muslim soldiers contributed their own wealth to join the army. There were, in fact, many Muslims left in Madinah who were keen to go but had neither provisions nor rides.

The news of the Muslim army advance reached the Romans. They were not yet fully prepared for a war. They could hardly believe that an Arab army had marched to Syria. "Muhammad must be a very strong emperor," they thought. The generals had once faced Khalid, Rasulullah's general. They did not want to face Rasulullah(S) himself. They withdrew their forces from Syria.

The Muslim army went as far as Tabuk in Syria. Rasulullah(S) stayed there for a few days. Many Arab tribes and small states which paid tribute to the Romans came to Rasulullah(S) for help. Roman taxes were high, there was no system of justice, and the Roman army was cruel. These Arab Christian rulers now came under the protection of Rasulullah's just rule. Their states became tributary states of Madinah.

Rasulullah(S) came back with a great victory. Now all these weak-minded Muslims came to Rasulullah(S) asking for forgiveness. They were truly repentant. They had realized their mistake. Rasulullah(S) said, "You have defied not my orders but Allah's orders. Only Allah can forgive you." Some of these Muslims were asked by Rasulullah(S) to stay away from everyone else. Some other Muslims tied themselves with the ropes of *Masjid al-Nabi* and said, "We shall not untie ourselves until Allah forgives us.".

Later when Allah forgave them Rasulullah(S) himself freed them from their chains and announed that Allah liked the sincerity of these Muslims and had forgiven them. It was a day of great happiness for them.

As for the *Munafiqun*, Allah had told His Prophet about their conspiracies. Abdullah bin Ubai fell sick at this time. Rasulullah(S) went to inquire about his health. He was on his death bed. He requested Rasulullah(S) to bury him in Rasulullah's own shirt. Rasulullah(S) accepted his request. After his death, Rasulullah(S) even said prayers for his soul. Later Allah sent a *Wahi* which completely forbade prayer for the *Munafiqun*. The *Wahi* said,

> O Muhammad, never pray for him if one of them dies,
> nor stand by his grave. Indeed, they disbelieved in Allah and
> His messenger and died while they were evildoers.
>
> *Surah* 9:84

Allah told the Prophet(S) not to follow a lenient policy with the *Munafiqun* any more.

Allah informed Rasulullah(S) about the *Masjid* of *al-Dirar* that was built to harm the Muslims. Rasulullah(S) was asked by Allah to raze this *Masjid* to the ground, which he did. Thus ended the conspiracies of the *Munafiqun*. Many of them now realized their mistakes. They came to Rasulullah(S) and asked his forgiveness and professed Islam sincerely. Rasulullah(S) accepted their apologies and prayed to Allah to make their faith in Islam strong.

Points of Review:

* The Muslims achieved great victories against the powerful Romans.

* Allah asked Rasulullah(S) to demolish the *Masjid al-Dirar* of the *Munafiqun*.

* Many *Munafiqun* repented and became good Muslims.

Words to Remember:
Repentent, tributary

Names to Remember:

Abdullah bin Rawahah, Abdullah bin Ubai, Jafar (R), Khalid bin Walid(R), *Masjid al-Dirar*, Mu'tah, Shurjil, Tabuk

81

The Quranic Study

1. *Surah Tawbah* was revealed by Allah which dealt with the *Ghazwah* of Tabuk and its aftermath. 9:38-72 was revealed before and 9:73-129 was revealed after the *Ghazwah* of Tabuk. With the background of this chapter, read these two sections with the help of following guide and understand their central ideas.

   a. The Muslims who followed Rasulullah(S) enthusiastically 9:44, 71, 88, 89, 99, 100, 111, 112, 119.

   b. The sincere Muslims who could not join the army due to lack of animals to ride or poor health, 9:91-93.

   c. Sincere Muslims who did not join due to laziness but repented to Allah, 9:102-105, 117, 118.

   d. *Munafiqun* who now started seeing the truth, 9:106

   e. *Munafiqun*, 9:38, 39, 42-49, 79, 81-89, 101.

   f. The Arabs of the desert who wanted to wait to see the results of the war before joining the Muslims, 9:97-98. 120, 121.

2. A *Masjid* is a place built to worship Allah alone. Such was *Masjid al-Quba*. The *Masjid* of *Munafiqun* is called *Masjid al-Dirar* because it was built to unite the mischievous. See how the Quran describes the two *Masjids*. 9:107-110.

3. It is obligatory for each community of Muslim *Ummah* to support a group of scholars of religion whose total life should be committed to the study, understanding and teaching of religion.

   Read *Surah al-Tawbah* 9:122.

   What is your community doing to respond to this call of Allah?

LESSON 21

AN APPEAL OF ISLAM

8th to 10th Year of Hijrah

We have already seen in the previous discussion how the Treaty of Hudaibiyah had paved the way for the peaceful spread of Islam. The liberation of Makkah, the victory of Hunain and the success of Tabuk further facilitated the peaceful spread of Islam through the missions of *Tabligh*. Rasulullah(S) continued to send the *Muballighun* (the preachers) to Arab tribes. Many Arab tribes wanted to learn the teachings of Islam. The *Muballighun* and teachers were invited by these tribes.

More and more Arab tribesmen from near and far wished to visit Rasulullah (S) and spend time with him. The first *Wafd* (delegation, plural *Wufoud*) to arrive in Madinah was as early as 5 A.H. It was from the tribe of *Muzainah*. The *Wafd* had four hundred members. They returned with the gift of Islam and a very special gift from Rasulullah(S), the dates from Madinah.

Between 8 and 10 A.H. began the rush of *Wufoud* to Madinah. Some of them were invited by Rasulullah(S), and others came on their own initiative. These *Wufoud* consisted of the tribesmen from diverse social backgrounds. Some came from distant cities where rich cultures had flourished, others came from *Bedouin* tribes who possessed neither fine culture nor much knowledge. Their motives were as varied as their background. Some, due to the love of Rasulullah(S) and Islam, came to seek further guidance from Rasulullah and enjoy the *Barakah* (the blessings) of his company; others came with the pride of *Jahiliyyah* seeking concessions for their people from the Islamic state of Madinah and hoping to accept Islam on their own terms. Also, among the people who came were both the Arab pagans and the Christians.

Banu Tamim was a prominent tribe, famous for its warriors, poets and speakers. They came to Madinah with the pride of *Jahiliyyah* and brought their poets, speakers and judges to demonstrate to Rasulullah(S) their superiority in the well known Arab arts of poetry and speech. They had hoped to win the respect of Muslims and a special status in Muslim society because of this.

83

Rasulullah(S) accepted their challenge. A contest was held for poetry and speech. The speech of Thabit bin Qais(R), and the spontaneous composition of Hassan bin Thabit(R), demonstrated the superiority of Islam and its messenger. *Banu Tamim* soon recognized the fact that superiority in Islam lies in submitting to Allah and His Prophet and following the teachings of Islam. As faith entered their hearts, they lost pride in their race and tribal past, and all of them accepted Islam.

The tribe of *Banu Sa'd* decided to send Zamam bin Tha'labah, their wise and experienced leader, to find out about the Prophet(S) and his teachings. They had, perhaps believed that the common people of their tribe should not be exposed to the influence of Rasulullah(S) before their leader finds out about him. Zamam rode his camel up to the open yard of *Masjid al-Nabi* with great pride. Rasulullah(S) was seated on the floor of the *Masjid* with his *Sahabah*(R). He was hardly distinguishable from them. Zamam had to ask, "Which one of you is Muhammad?"

A *Sahabi*(R) pointed out Rasulullah(S). Zamam approached and addressed him, "O, son of Abdul Muttalib! I will ask you a few questions. I will be frank and to the point. Do not be offended."

Rasulullah(S) replied calmly, "Ask whatever you wish to ask." Zamam asked Rasulullah(S) about the teachings of Islam and his mission as a messenger. The speech of Rasulullah(S) convinced him of the truth of Rasulullah's mission. He accepted Islam and returned home, determined to invite his tribe to the path of Islam. Upon arrival he addressed his people about the evils of idolatry and the virtues of Islam. Such was the force of his preaching that by evening the entire tribe had accepted Islam.

In Yemen the tribe of *Ash'arin* had received the call of Islam through its poet, Tufail Dusi(R). Its delegation returned to Madinah singing songs full of love for Rasulullah(S). They stayed with Rasulullah(S), received their Islamic education and returned to Yemen to work for Islam. The famous *Sahabi* Abu Mousa Ash'ari(R) belonged to this tribe.

Tufail Dusi (R) had worked hard to invite his own clan of *Dus* to Islam, but this clan continued to resist. Tufail(R) was so sincerely fervent in his belief that the resistance of *Dus* irritated and angered him. The clan respected him for his wisdom and poetry, but would not listen to him in this matter. He warned them, in vain, of the evil consequences of their defiance. Tufail(R), in disappointment, left for Madinah and reported his difficulties to Rasulullah(S). Rasulullah(S) loved Tufail(R) and appreciated his zeal, but he also knew that Tufail(R) had a hot temper. He advised Tufail(R), "Invite your people to Islam with kindness and gentle pursuasion and not with anger and threats." He also prayed for the conversion of Tufail's tribe.

When Tufail(R) returned to *Dus* his clan responded to his call enthusiastically. They accepted Islam, and 80 families made *Hijrah* to Madinah in order to live with Rasulullah(S) and his *Sahabah*(R). Among the *Muhajirun* was Abu Huraira(R), famous narrator of *Ahadith* (traditions).

The *Banu Hars bin Ka'b* was a noble tribe of Najran. It was well known for its chivalry and innumerable victories over its enemies. The tribe accepted Islam through the *Tabligh* efforts of Khalid bin Walid(R). Rasulullah(S) had sent a special invitation to them to visit Madinah. They came under the leadership of Qais bin al Hasin(R). Rasulullah(S) welcomed them warmly and asked them, "Tell me what has made you victorious over your enemies?"

They answered, "Our unity and sense of justice." This answer delighted Rasulullah(S) greatly because Islam also teaches unity and justice based upon *Taqwah* (fear of Allah). Rasulullah (S) appointed Qais(R) the chief of his tribe.

The tribe of *Tay* was another famous tribe of Yemen. It had two chiefs, Zaid al-Khil and Adi bin Hatim. They had separate domains and ruled independently in their respective areas. Zaid was known for his generosity and horsemanship. He came to Rasulullah(S) with some selected and influential members of his tribe. Rasulullah(S) received them and explained to them the teachings of Islam. Within a short time they accepted Islam.

Rasulullah(S) always advised his *Sahabah*(R) to give their children good names. The children grow up imbibing the characteristics of the meaning of their names. When a *Kafir* accepted Islam, and Rasulullah(S) found his name either opposed to the teachings of Islam or not meaningful, he selected an appropriate name for him. For Zaid-*al-Khail*, (Zaid, the horseman), Rasulullah(S) chose Zaid-*al-Khair*, (Zaid, the generous). Zaid was very happy to receive this honor, and he lived up to his name in the service of Islam.

The other chief of *Tay* was 'Adi, son of the famous Hatim Ta'i. Among the Arabs, name of Hatim was synonymous with charity, generosity and hospitality. 'Adi was a pious christian and a worthy son of his famous father. He commanded a great respect among his people. When a Muslim army entered the land of Tay 'Adi fled to Syria. Not knowing the tolerance of Islam and Muslims, he was afraid for his life and religion. His sister, however, was taken a prisoner of war and brought to Rasulullah(S). When Rasulullah(S) learned about her family and her father he showed her special consideration and allowed her to leave for Syria to join her brother. She went to Syria and told her brother about the generosity and kindness of Rasulullah(S). She convinced him that with Muhammad(S) both his life and religion would be safe.

'Adi could not resist the pursuasion of his sister and arrived at *Masjid al-Nabi*. Rasulullah(S) was very pleased to receive him and showed him his personal love. He invited 'Adi to visit his home. On their way, Rasulullah(S) met an old lady. He stopped, and listened to the conversation of this commoner with attention and patience. 'Adi was a chief, and had seen the courts of Caesers and their kings. He had never seen a chief or king as considerate as Rasulullah(S). He was deeply impressed by Rasulullah's humility.

When he visited Rasulullah's home he was amazed by the simplicity of the Prophet's life. He opened his heart to accept Islam. "Muhammad(S) is not an ordinary king," he realized. "He is the Prophet of Allah. He has come, not to establish his empire, but to establish the kingdom of Allah on earth." 'Adi became a Muslim. Soon the entire tribe of *Tay* accepted Islam.

Banu Thaqif of Ta'if had resisted the Muslim army successfully and continued to defy Islam. Rasulullah(S) had prayed for their guidance. Two years later *Banu Thaqif* sent a powerful delegation to Madinah to negotiate for them a special position in Islam. Rasulullah(S) received them with great hospitality and allowed them to put their tents in the courtyard of *Masjid al-Nabi*. For several days, *Banu Thaqif* continued to observe the Muslims and to learn from Rasulullah(S) about Islam. Finally, they showed willingness to accept Islam on the condition that they should be allowed to have the freedom to practice usury, drink alcohol and commit adultery. Rasulullah(S) rejected those terms. The principles of Islam are divine. No one, including the Prophet(S) himself, had any power to alter them.

Then *Banu Thaqif* asked Rasulullah(S) about their idol, *al-Lat*. Rasulullah(S) told them that it would be broken. The tribe reluctantly accepted the fact, but requested that some-one from outside their tribe be sent to break the idol. Some of them still believed that al-Lat had the power to destroy anyone who angered it.

Rasulullah(S) understood their reluctance and accepted their excuse. He knew that once they had seen the helplessness of their idol, their superstitions would disappear.

Finally, *Banu Taqif* wanted exemptions from *Salat, Zakat* and *Jihad*. Rasulullah (S) refused all that. He only agreed that they would not **destroy** their idols by their own hands

Rasulullah(S) sent two *Sahabah*, Abu Sufyan(R) and Mughira bin Sha'bah(R) to destroy the idols of *Banu Thaqif*. As the *Sahabah*(R) arrived to break the idols, some tribesmen felt terror in their hearts. Women began crying for their gods, and children watched with amazement. *Al-Lat* was broken into pieces. With it was broken the pride and superstition of the days of *Jahiliyyah*.

The tribe of *Banu Asad* was a proud ally of the *Quraish*. They had accepted Islam in 5 A.H., but had not received the training of Rasulullah(S). In 9 A.H., they took the initiative to send a *Wafd* to Rasulullah(S). They felt, by accepting Islam and coming to Rasulullah(S), they had favoured him and should have something in return for this favor. As they met Rasulullah(S), they told him, "See, we have come to you on our own initiative. You did not send any invitation to us." Rasulullah(S) did not answer them, but Allah sent a *Wahi* which spoke,

> They impress on you that they have accepted Islam.
> Tell them, "Count not the acceptance of Islam as
> a favor upon me; no, on the other hand, Allah
> has guided you to the Faith, if you are sincere.
> *al-Hujurat 49:17*

Banu Asad immediately realized their mistake and thanked Allah for taking them out of the darkness of *Kufr* to the light of Islam.

Ash'ath bin Qais, the leader of the affluent *Kindah* tribe, led his own tribe's *Wafd* to Madinah. The *Wafd* of *Kindah* had eighty horsemen. They wore expensive robes and covered them with artistic silken shawls made in *Hira*. As Rasulullah(S) received them, he was surprised by their clothes. He asked the *Wafd*, "Have you not accepted Islam yet?

"Yes, we have," they replied.

"What are these silken shawls on your shoulders?" Rasulullah(S) asked, reminding them of the simplicity of a Muslim.

They realized that silk is forbidden for a Muslim. The delegation took off their expensive shawls, tore them and threw them on the ground, showing their complete submission to the commandments of Allah.

Not everyone, who came, was ready to accept Islam. Some of them recognizing the rising power of Islam, came only to secure convenient terms. The tribe of *Banu 'Amir* was led by its leaders 'Amir bin Tufail, Arbad bin Qais and Jabbar bin Salma. They were not sincere in their faith and they came determined either to receive concessions from Rasulullah(S) or to kill him. They chose 'Amir as their leader to represent their interests. They planned, that while 'Amir engaged Rasulullah(S) in conversation, Arbad should attack him and kill him. 'Amir showed false respect to Rasulullah(S) by speaking to him politely. Rasulullah(S), however, was well aware of their attitude and stopped them from such hypocritic politeness. He demanded that they should speak frankly and state their intention clearly.

'Amir, then, presented his terms, "O, Muhammad! You may rule the village while I will rule the city, or you may rule both but nominate me as your successor. If you reject my terms, I will invade Madinah with my tribe and allies." Rasulullah(S) was fully aware of his intentions. He rejected these terms. 'Amir now expected Arbad and Jabbar to attack Rasulullah(S), but was stunned to see Arbad and Jabbar trembling with fear. 'Amir and Arbad left the Prophet(S) in frustration. Jabbar and other members of this *Wafd* experienced a change in them and stayed with Rasululah(S). Rasulullah(S) prayed to Allah, "O, Allah! Save me from the mischief of these people." After a few days both 'Amir and Arbad died of plague.

Jabbar and the rest of the *Wafd* were so impressed by Rasulullah(S) and his teachings, that they accepted Islam and returned to their tribe to teach them their new faith.

An important *Wafd* to visit Madinah was from the Christians of *Najran*. Rasulullah(S) had invited them to visit Madinah and accept Islam. The Christian state of *Najran* was under the sovereignty of Rome. They had a huge church and they called it Ka'bah. It was under an archbishop. They did not accept

Islam but agreed to send a high powered delegation to visit the Prophet(S) under the leadership of its archbishop. These people had hoped that they could convert the Prophet(S) to their religion. The *Wafd* was received very kindly and Rasulullah (S) allowed them to stay in *Masjid al-Nabi*. They were allowed to perform Christian worship in the *Masjid* when the time of worship came for them. During their stay, they asked Rasulullah(S), many questions. Allah sent a *Wahi* (*Ali Imran* 3:1-80) to answer their questions. The *Wahi* invited them to join Islam,

> Say, O People of the Book! Come to an agreement between
> us and you, that we shall worship none except Allah,
> that we associate no partners with Him, that none
> of us shall take anyone for Lord besides Allah. If
> they turn away, then tell them, "Bear witness that
> we are Muslims."

> *Ali 'Imran* 3:64

Rasulullah recited this verse to them. The Christians replied,"How can we accept the faith, when we are already believers?"

Rasulullah(S) replied, "But you worship the cross, and call Isa(S) the son of God. How could you be a believer?" Many long conversations between Rasulullah(S) and the Christians took place but Christians did not change their minds. They continued to doubt the truth of Rasulullah's mission. Then Allah sent a *Wahi* (3:61) and asked Rasulullah to invite them for *Mubahilah*. In *Mubahilah* both Rasulullah(S) and the Christians would come out with their families and invite the wrath of Allah upon those, who practised falsehood and told lies. Thus the curse of Allah descends upon those whose belief is false. Some Christians seemed willing to accept this. Rasulullah(S) came out with his daughter, Fatimah(R) and grandsons, Hasan(R) and Husain(R). The Christians discussed the situation among them. One wise priest advised them, "If Muhammad is truly the prophet of Allah, then we shall be destroyed. It is better not to have *Mubahilah*."

The *Wafd* of *Najran* neither accepted Islam nor the challenge of *Mubahilah*. However, they accepted the political sovereignty of Madinah. Rasulullah(S) offered them very generous terms and allowed them to continue to practise their religion, maintain their churches, and enjoy full freedom.

The *Wufoud* continued to arrive in Madinah till the last days of Rasulullah's life. Many of them had received no training in Islam. They were simple nomads. They did not know how to behave in the presence of Rasulullah(S). Allah sent *Wahi (Surah al-Hujurat* 49:1-11) with specific teachings of social etiquettes and manners for the Muslims.

Islam was now a powerful force in Arabia. Every day tribe after tribe was accepting Islam.

We have learned

* Between 5 A.H. and 10 A.H., many *Wufoud* of the Arabs came to Madinah to accept Islam.

* The *Wafd* of the Christians of *Najran* did not accept Islam and Rasulullah(S) allowed them to practise their religion and maintain their churches.

* Allah taught important social lessons to the Muslims through revelations.

Words to Remember
Muballigh, Muballighun, Tabligh, Wafd, **Wufoud**

Quranic Study
Surah al-Hujurat, 49, taught the Muslims important social etiquettes and manners.

1. For Muslims' behavior towards the Prophet(S) read: 49:1 - Respect in the presence of the Prophet(S)
   49:3 - Manner of Conversation
   49:5 - Meeting with Rasulullah(S)

2. Rules for an Islamic social living:
   49:6 - Verification of news.
   49:9,10 - Peace among Muslim groups
   49:11 - Not to laugh at, ridicule, or defame another person.
   49:12 - Avoid suspicion, spying and speaking ill of others.

3. For the Arabs, who wanted favors from Rasulullah(S) because of their race, tribe, social status and wealth, the Quran taught:
   49:7, 17 - Allah's favor to Muslims
   49:13—15 - Human equality and a new basis of Divine preference.

LESSON 22

HAJJATUL WADA' (FAREWELL PILGRIMAGE)
Tenth Year of *Hijrah*

Islam now was the dominant power in Arabia. In Madinah, the community of Islam succeeded in defeating the *Kuffar*, the Jews and the *Munafiqun*. Muslims in Arabia were now one community. Their tribal differences were no longer important. Their longstanding disputes were forgotten. The former enemies were now united into a brotherhood of true faith. All of them worshipped Allah and believed in Rasulullah(S) as their Prophet. They said *Salat* five times a day, kept *Sawm* in *Ramadan*, performed *Hajj* and gave regular *Zakat*. Their morals and manners had no likeness to their earlier life in *Jahiliyyah*.

A decade before, no one could have believed except pious Muslims, that the divided, uneducated, and vice ridden Arabs would become a great moral force. They would start a new era in human history.

Rasulullah (S) was in the sixty-third year of his life. He declared his intention to go on pilgrimage. The news spread fast throughout Muslim lands and people from far and near started moving toward Kabah. Each one wanted to be blessed by the company of their beloved Prophet (S). Little did they know that it was a farewell pilgrimage for Rasulullah(S) before his final journey to eternal life.

Thousands of Muslims accompanied Rasulullah(S). They left saying *Talbiah*,

> O Allah, we respond to Your call.
> We respond to Your call, there is no partner with You.
> All priases and blessingss are Yours. All sovereignty belongs to You.
> O Allah, we respond to Your call.

When Rasulullah (S) reached Makkah, one hundred fourteen thousand people were with him. Many more joined him in Makkah and on the way to *Arafat* for the performance of *Hajj*.

In the last day of the *Hajj* in the vast open field of *Arafat* on 9th *Dhul Hijjah*, Rasulullah (S) stood up and gave the famous *Khutba* (sermon) which is truly the first declaration of human rights. He spoke as hundreds and thousands of people listened intently with love and devotion.

All priases are due to Allah. We glorify Him and seek His help and pardon.

O people! Listen to what I say. I think I shall not be able to meet with you at this place ever after this year.

O people! Your blood, your property, and your honor is sacred and to be respected.

You will meet Allah and be answerable for your actions. Neither the son is responsible for the crimes of the father, nor the father for the crimes of his son.

Listen! All Muslims are brothers to each other. You will not oppress one another. The blood revenge of the days of old is abolished.

The usury is being ended.

Fear Allah concerning your women. You have certain rights over your women, and your women have certain rights over you. Lay injunction upon your women but kindly.

O people! Obey your *Amir* (leader). Even if a black Abyssinian slave be your leader, obey him as long as he follows the Book of Allah.

O people! The child belongs to the marriage bed. Allah has fixed a share in his inheritance. He who attributes his ancestry to other than his own father, Allah's curse will fall on him.

Listen! I have left among you the Book of Allah and my *Sunnah*. Hold fast to it. You will never go astray.

Then he looked at the poeple and asked them, "When asked about me what will you say to Allah?" All the people replied together, "You have brought us the message. You have fulfilled the mission."

Rasulullah(S) looked up to heaven and said, "O Allah, be my witness." Then he repeated it three times. Rasulullah(S) combined his *Zuhr* and *Asr* prayer in *Arafat*. After *Asr* he left for *Muzdalifah*. The crowd was large. Everyone wanted to come close to him to see him and talk to him. As he rode the camel he appealed to people, "Be patient O people, be patient."

In *Muzdalifah*, Rasulullah (S) said his *Maghrib* and *Isha* prayer., then he went to sleep. He did not wake up for *Tahajjud* as was his habit. He said *Fajr* prayer before sunrise and left for *Mina*.

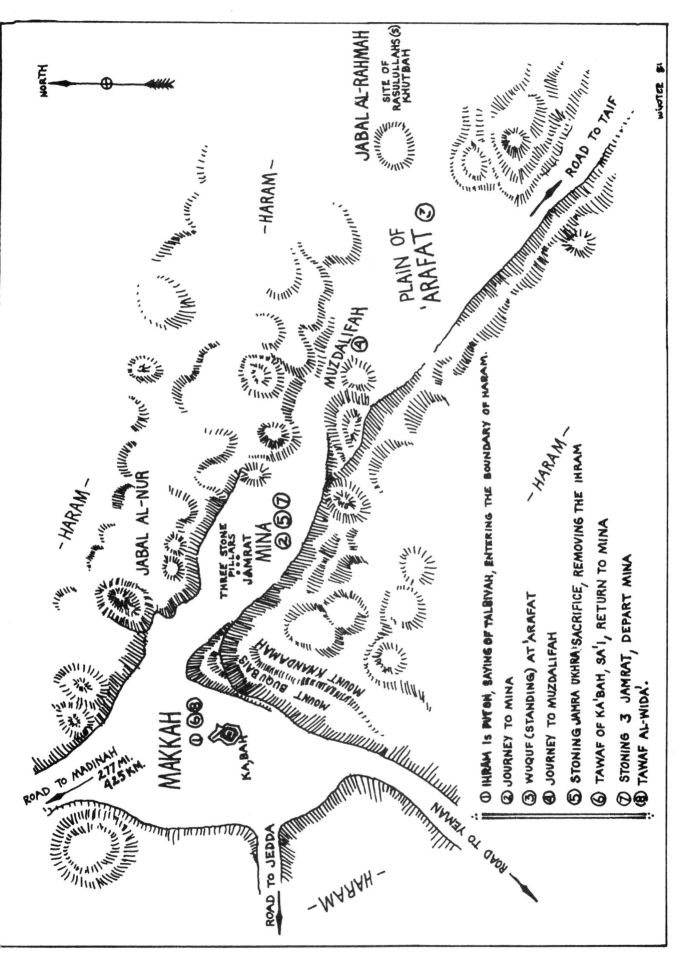

NORTH

JABAL AL-RAHMAH
SITE OF RASULULLAHS (S) KHUTBAH

PLAIN OF 'ARAFAT ③

ROAD TO TAIF

WINTER 81

MUZDALIFAH ④

HARAM

HARAM

HARAM

JABAL AL-NUR

THREE STONE PILLARS
JAMRAT
MINA ②⑤⑦

MOUNT KHANDAMAH

MOUNT BUQU BAIS

MAKKAH ①⑥⑧

KA'BAH

ROAD TO MADINAH 277 MI. 425 KM.

ROAD TO JEDDA

ROAD TO YEMAN

HARAM

:: ——————————————————— ·:·

① IHRAM IS PUT ON, SAYING OF TALBIYAH, ENTERING THE BOUNDARY OF HARAM.
② JOURNEY TO MINA
③ WUQUF (STANDING) AT 'ARAFAT
④ JOURNEY TO MUZDALIFAH
⑤ STONING JAMRA UKHRA, SACRIFICE, REMOVING THE IHRAM
⑥ TAWAF OF KA'BAH, SA'I, RETURN TO MINA
⑦ STONING 3 JAMRAT, DEPART MINA
⑧ TAWAF AL-WIDA'.

PLAN OF THE HAJJ

93

He told people, "Learn the method of *Hajj* from me. I may not be able to make another *Hajj* next year." On his way people kept on asking questions and he went on replying to them.

The next day on the 10th of *Dhul Hijjah*, he addressed the Muslims again and said,

> I tell you, each one of you should respect the life and property of each other just as you have respect for this sacred day, for this sacred month, and for this sacred city.

> Be kind to your slaves, feed and clothe them as you do to yourself. They are the servants of Allah and should not be punished.

On the eleventh *Dhul Hijjah*, Rasulullah(S) spoke to his *Sahabah*(R) once again. After praising Allah he said,

> O people!
> Your Lord is one.
> Your father Adam is one
> Adam was created from clay.

> Remember!

> There is no superiority to an Arab over a non-Arab
> and a non-Arab over an Arab.
> Nor white over black or black over white
> except in piety.

> Allah says, "Noblest in the eyes of Allah are those who are the most righteous¹.

> Behold!
> Those who are present have a responsibility to give the message to those who are not present.

Then he lifted up his head and looked towards Heaven and said,

> O Allah, bear witness, I have conveyed the message.

It was at this time that Allah sent His *Wahi* informing Muhammad(S) about the completion of his mission. Rasulullah(S) immediately announced it,

¹*al-Hujurat* 49:13

94

Millions of Muslims have followed the path of Rasulullah(S) to the valley of Arafat and prayed under *Jabal al-Rahmah*.

This day I have perfected for you your religion, and completed my favor upon you. And I am well pleased with Islam as your religion.

al-Ma'idah, 5:3

Muslims were very happy to receive this verse. But Abu Bakr (R) understood well that Rasulullah's mission was now completed. The purpose of his prophethood was fulfilled and his physical presence would not remain much longer in this world. This thought made him sad.

Rasulullah(S) and his party returned to Madinah and the other Muslims went back to their cities.

Points of Review:

* Rasulullah(S) performed *Hajjatul Wada'* with a large number of Muslims.

* In the plains of Arafat, he gave his last sermon.

* A *Wahi* confirmed that Allah had chosen al-Islam as His religion and completed the mission of Rasulullah(S).

Words to Remember:

Hajjatul Wada', human rights, longstanding, *Khutba*, sovereignty, vice-ridden.

Names to Remember

Arafat, Mina, Muzdalifah

Quranic Study

Hajj is one of the five *Arkan* of Islam. It is a unique experience which strength_ ens the bonds of Islamic fraternity and the *Ummah's* relationship with Allah. Rasulullah(S) in his *Hajjatul Wada'*, himself demonstrated the proper method of performing *Hajj*. To understand the true significance of this Islamic *rukn*, read the following verses of the Quran.

1) *al-Baqarah* 2:158. *Safa* and *Marwa* are signs of Allah.
2) *al-Baqarah* 2:197-203. The spirit of the *Hajj*.
3) *Ali 'Imran* 3:96, 97. The Kabah, the first house of Allah.
4) *al-Hajj* 22:26. Establishment of the Kabah.
5) *al-Hajj* 22:27-29 the universality of the *Hajj*.
6) *al-Hajj* 22:30-33 The meaning of the *Hajj*.

THE FINAL JOURNEY TO ETERNAL LIFE

After *Hajjatul Wada'* there was every indication that Rasulullah(S) was making final preparation to meet Allah and rest in peace in Paradise. On his return to Madinah, *Surah al-Nasr* was revealed to him which said,

> When Allah's help and victory comes,
> and you see the people entering the religion of Allah in crowds,
> Then celebrate the praises of your Lord;
> and pray for forgiveness.
> For He is Oft-returning (through His grace and mercy)
>
> *al-Nasr, 110.*

Rasulullah(S) thereafter spent most of his time in prayer and *Dhikr* of Allah (Remembering Allah).In his last *Ramadan* three months before his *Hajj*, he spent twenty days in *I'tikaf*(seclusion and prayer). He recited the whole Quran twice to Jibril(A).When he returned after the *Hajj*, he went to the graves of the *Shuhada* of *Uhud* and bid them farewell.His prayers for *Shuhada'* were so moving, as if from a man about to die, saying farewell to the living. Then he went to *Masjid al-Nabi* and spoke to the *Sahabah (R)*.

> I am going to the river of *Kawthar* ahead of you. I will make arrangements for your reception and be a witness for your actions.

> I see with my eyes the keys of the treasures of earth given to me. Allah is my witness, I don't fear that my *Ummah* will commit shirk but I fear that you may get involved in the greed of this world and start killing each other. Then you may be destroyed like the earlier nations.

One night, on the 18th or 19th of *Safar*, 11 A.H., Rasulullah(S) went to *Jannat al-Baqi'*, the graveyard of Muslims in Madinah to say *Du'a*, as if he was saying farewell to those who died before him. He told his servant, Abu Muhaibah, "I have been given a choice: to have the keys of the treasures of the world until the end of time, and then go and meet the Lord; or I may immediately go and meet the Lord."

His servant said, "May my parents be sacrificed on you. Accept the keys of the treasures of the world and then go to Paradise."

Rasulullah(S) replied, "No, I have already made my choice. I have decided to meet my Lord."

The next day, on Wednesday, he developed a headache and a high temperature. As five days passed, he continued his daily visits to his wives. But now he felt weak. He got permission from his wives to stay in the room of A'isha(R). Though weak and exhausted, he contined to lead the prayer and meet the *Sahabah* and the visitors. When it became impossible for him to move he asked his *Sahabi* and old friend, Abu Bakr (R), to be *Imam* (leader) for the *Salat.*

One day, he went to the *Masjid* with the help of Ali(R) and Abbas(R). He led the prayer while he was seated. He was helped on the *Mimbar* (dias) and talked to the *Sahabah(R).* Though exhausted and weak, he made his last address to his *Sahabah (R).*

> Allah has given His servant a choice to choose the pleasures of this world or of hereafter. He has chosen the **Hereafter**. The person for whose friendship and wealth I am most grateful is Abu Bakr.

> Other nations had made the graves of their prophets objects of worship. Remember you don't fall into that error.

> O people! I want to advise you to be kind to the *Ansar.* Other people will increase but the number of *Ansar* will decrease. They have fulfilled their duty to Islam. Now you have to fulfill your responsibilities toward them.

Rasulullah(S) learned that some people had raised objections to the command of young Usamah, son of Zaid, the freed slave. He told the people,

> If some of you today are raising objections on the leadership of Usamah, they did so earlier also in the case of his father, Zaid. By Allah! Zaid was the most deserving of that position and dearest to me. After him, Usamah is the most deserving for this position and dearest to me.

Thus he struck finally at the long established ideas of preference for the family status and seniority. In Islam neither family nor age should be a factor for holding a responsible position, but only one's competence.

One day his condition became worse. In that condition he remembered that he had seven *Dinars*. He asked A'ishah(R) to distribute them to the poor. He said, "Muhammad does not want to meet his Lord in embarrassment."

One day he advised his daughter, Fatimah(R), and his aunt, Safiyah(R), "Do good deeds. Only your deeds will help you before Allah. Nothing helps you before Allah but your own deeds."

Rasulullah's advice made it clear that family ties, status or birth cannot save anyone. Each one of us has been given a "will" to act and is responsible for his own deeds.

Due to Rasulullah's sickness, there was general sadness in Madinah. Abu Bakr(R) led the prayers. People were so used to Rasulullah(S) that life without his presence looked meaningless. The *Ansar* and *Muhajirun* could not suppress their tears when they thought of the days when every day they enjoyed the company of Rasulullah(S).

One morning, he woke up extremely weak. He stood with A'ishah's support and lifted the curtain. *Fajr* (morning) *Salat* was being said. Rasulullah(S) had a smile of satisfaction on his face. When the *Sahabah*(R) heard the movement of the curtain, the *Salat* was disturbed. They became restless when they saw Rasulullah(S). He asked them to continue their prayer. This was his last glimpse of his *Ummah*. He could see with satisfaction how the message of Allah would continue after him.

His condition worsened during the day. He kept on praying, "O Allah, help me in the hour of death." He was half conscious but was still advising his *Ummah*, "Safeguard your *Salat* Be kind to your slaves."

He looked up to heaven and said, "Allah indeed is the best companion."

Having fulfilled his mission and having watched its success he left this temporary house for the eternal house in Heaven. He shall wait for his *Ummah* on the river of *Kawthar* and shall be our *Shafi'* (intercessor) before Allah. "There is no doubt, that you will die (one day)," the Quran declares, " indeed, they will also die." al-Zumr 39:30. "Inna li Allahi wa inna ilaihi raji'un." "We belong to Allah and shall return to Him." (al-Baqarah 2:156).

Points to Review:

* In his last days, Rasulullah (S) was informed by *Wahi* that he should now spend more time in prayer.

* Until he breathed his last, he remained concerned for his *Ummah.*

* His last words were, "Allah indeed is the best friend."

Words to Remember:

I'tikaf, Shafi

Names to Remember:

Abu Bakr (R), A'ishah (R), Fatimah (R), *Jannat al Baqi'
Kawthar,* Safiyah(R) Usamah, son of Zaid(R).

The Quranic Study

The message of Islam, which Allah revealed through many Prophets, was finally completed through Rasulullah(S).

1.   Islam is the only religion acceptable to Allah. *Ali Imran* 3:19, 85; *al-Ma'idah* 5:3; *al-Hajj* 22:78

ii.   It is a mercy from Allah that He chose Islam for us. Read *al-An'am* 6:125; *al-Zumr* 39:22; *al-Hujurat* 49:17

iii.   Islam means complete surrender to the Will of Allah. Read *al-Baqarah* 2:112, 208; *Ali 'Imran* 3:102.

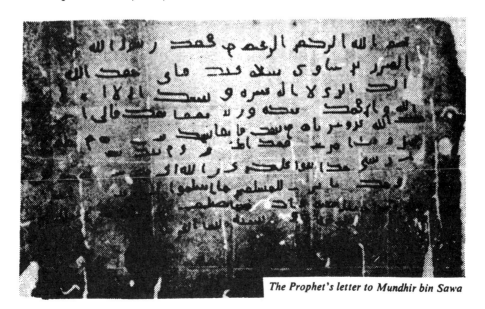

The Prophet's letter to Mundhir bin Sawa

LESSON 24

THE MISSION CONTINUES

The news of the death of Rasulullah (S) apread throughout Madinah. The *Sahabah(R)* were so used to his presence that they could not believe he was gone. The way they loved the Prophet(S) no one has ever loved any one. In that hour of greatest sorrow, they could not think what that tragedy meant.

Umar(R) got so angry hearing the news that he threatened death to those who uttered such words. He said, "Rasulullah could not die. He has gone to meet Allah and will come back."

Abu Bakr(R) was also in a state of shock. He was also very close to Rasulullah (S). He also benefitted fully from the spiritual training of Rasulullah (S). He was first to go to visit Rasulullah's body. He kissed him on the forehead. Then he came out and addressed the grieving *Sahabah(R)*. "Those of you who worshipped Muhammad, remember, Muhammad(S) is dead. Whoever amongst you worshipped Allah, remember, Allah is alive and eternal.

Then he recited the verse from the Quran,
> Muhammad is no more than a messenger. Many messengers passed away before this. If he died or was killed, will you then turn back on your heels. Not the least harm will he do to Allah. But Allah on the other hand always rewards those people who are grateful to Him.
> *Ali-'Imran 3:144*

Then he made an appeal to Muslims to continue the mission of Islam and have their faith in Allah. This speech calmed the people's sorrow.

Rasulullah(S) was buried in his beloved wife A'ishah's room where he died. To this day this sight is the center of devotion and love of millions of Muslims.

The closest *Sahabah* of Rasulullah(S), Abu Bakr(R) and Umar(R) later were also buried in this room with the permission of A'ishah(R).

Hundreds and thousands of Muslims visit Madinah, the city of Rasulullah (S), say their *Salat* in the *Masjid al-Nabi* offer *Salam* at Rasulullah's grave, and come back with renewed faith to continue the work of Islam.

May peace and Blessings of Allah always be with Him.*Amin.*

Allahumma Salli ala Sayyidina wa Mawlana Muhammadin wa Barik wa Sallim, Amin.

O Allah,

May your Peace be upon our leader and master Muhammad, and may your Blessing and Salutations be also with him. *Amin.*

Quranic Study

1. Islam did not establish a church or a priestly class to preach and administer religion, rather, the *Ummah* as a whole is given the responsibility of this special mission. Read:
   al-Baqarah 2:142; *Ali 'Imran* 3: 104. 110

2. The Quran describes the personal characteristics of the members of the Muslim *Ummah* in clear terms. Such Characteristics are to be found throughout the Quran. Read:
   al-Baqarah 2:2-5; *Ali Imran* 3:17; *al-Ahzab* 33:35

   These characteristics, which early Muslims developed, made them model missionaries of Islam.

Inscriptions from the Eski Cami, Edirne, in decorative Kufi, with a Prophetic *hadith* in thuluth, and the "Thron-verse" in squared Kufi.